PORTSMOUTH PUBLIC LIBRARY
175 PARROTT AVENUE
PORTSMOUTH, NH 03801-4452
603-427-1540   DEC 18 2017

O9-ABG-319

SUPER EARTH
ENCYCLOPEDIA

DK SMITHSONIAN

SUPER EARTH

ENCYCLOPEDIA

AUTHOR JOHN WOODWARD

SMITHSONIAN CONSULTANT JEFFERY E. POST, PH.D.

GENERAL CONSULTANT PROFESSOR IAIN STEWART

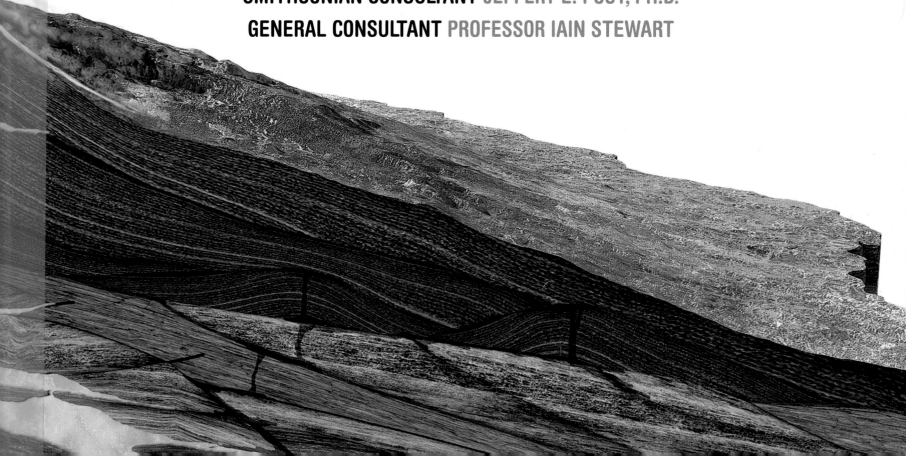

CONTENTS

 Penguin Random House

DK LONDON
Senior Editor Shaila Brown
US Editor Karyn Gerhard
Managing Editor Lisa Gillespie
Managing Art Editor Owen Peyton Jones
Producer, Pre-Production Gillian Reid
Senior Producer Anna Vallarino
Jacket Design Development Manager Sophia MTT
Jacket Editor Claire Gell

Jacket Designer Mark Cavanagh
Illustrator Arran Lewis
Publisher Andrew Macintyre
Art Director Karen Self
Associate Publishing Director Liz Wheeler
Design Director Phil Ormerod
Publishing Director Jonathan Metcalf

DK INDIA
Project Editor Nisha Shaw
Assistant Editor Smita Mathur
Managing Editor Rohan Sinha
Project Art Editor Vikas Chauhan

Art Editors Priyansha Tuli, Meenal Goel
Assistant Art Editors Rohit Bhardwaj, Devika Khosla
Managing Art Editor Arunesh Talapatra
Picture Researcher Deepak Negi
Picture Research Manager Taiyaba Khatoon
Jacket Designer Dhirendra Singh
Jacket Editorial Coordinator Priyanka Sharma
Managing Jacket Editor Sreshtha Bhattacharya
Senior DTP Designers Harish Aggarwal, Neeraj Bhatia
DTP Designer Sachin Gupta
Pre-Production Manager Balwant Singh
Production Manager Pankaj Sharma

First American Edition, 2017
Published in the United States by DK Publishing
345 Hudson Street, New York, New York 10014
Copyright © 2017 Dorling Kindersley Limited
DK, a Division of Penguin Random House LLC
17 18 19 20 21 10 9 8 7 6 5 4 3 2 1
001–289092–07/2017

All rights reserved.
Without limiting the rights under the copyright reserved above, no
part of this publication may be reproduced, stored in or introduced
into a retrieval system, or transmitted, in any form, or by any means
(electronic, mechanical, photocopying, recording, or otherwise),
without the prior written permission of the copyright owner.

Published in Great Britain by Dorling Kindersley Limited.
A catalog record for this book is available
from the Library of Congress.
ISBN: 978-1-4654-6187-2

DK books are available at special discounts when purchased in bulk
for sales promotions, premiums, fund-raising, or educational use.
For details, contact: DK Publishing Special Markets,
345 Hudson Street, New York, New York 10014
SpecialSales@dk.com
Printed and bound in China

A WORLD OF IDEAS:
SEE ALL THERE IS TO KNOW
www.dk.com

Smithsonian

THE SMITHSONIAN
Established in 1846, the Smithsonian—the world's largest
museum and research complex—includes 19 museums and galleries
and the National Zoological Park. The total number of artifacts,
works of art, and specimens in the Smithsonian's collection
is estimated at 154 million. The Smithsonian is a renowned
research center, dedicated to public education, national service,
and scholarship in the arts, sciences, and history.

INTRODUCTION

Earth is a dramatic, dynamic planet—a spectacular world of rock, water, air, and life that is in a constant state of change. Forces deep below the planet's surface drive slow but relentless movements of the rocky crust, which push up mountains, trigger earthquakes, and fuel volcanoes. Meanwhile, the heat of the Sun sets the atmosphere in motion, generating the wind and rain that wear away the landscape to create Earth's stunning landforms.

Super Earth Encyclopedia gives an enthralling insight into this fascinating natural drama. As well as showcasing the extraordinary geological wonders of the world, it probes deeper to explain the making and shaping of Earth. From the searing heat of volcanic lava on Hawaii to the frozen wastes of Antarctica, *Super Earth Encyclopedia* reveals our planet as a place of jaw-dropping beauty and wonder.

UNIQUE EARTH

Created from a cloud
of gas and dust more than
4.6 billion years ago, our world
has evolved into a uniquely
dynamic planet. Heat from
deep below its surface keeps
the crust in continuous
slow motion, so its pattern
of oceans and continents
is always changing.

EARTH IN SPACE

Planet Earth is one of the eight major planets that orbit our nearest star—the Sun. Along with many smaller objects, including dwarf planets, moons, asteroids, and comets, these planets make up our solar system. It is one of the countless systems of stars and orbiting planets in the universe. But as far as we know, Earth is the only planet that includes all the conditions required to create and support life.

Saturn, the second largest planet in the solar system, has spectacular icy rings that are visible from Earth. Like Jupiter, it has a huge family of moons and a stormy atmosphere.

SOLAR SYSTEM

When the Sun formed from a vast cloud of dust and gas about 4.6 billion years ago, some of this dust and gas was left over. It spread out as a spinning disc around the young Sun. Over time, most of it clumped together to form the planets of the solar system—the small inner rocky planets and the outer gas giants.

Our Sun is a medium-sized star—a vast ball of hot gas that lies at the center of the solar system. All the heat and light needed to sustain life on Earth comes from the Sun.

About 70 percent of Earth's surface is covered in water, while most of its land is divided into seven huge continents.

Mercury, the smallest of the rocky planets, has a surface similar to Earth's cratered Moon.

Mars is smaller and colder than Earth. The iron-rich rocks give Mars its distinctive rust-red tint.

Venus is covered with dense yellow clouds of acid. With a surface temperature of 860°F (460°C), it is the hottest planet in the solar system.

Inner planets

The four planets nearest to the Sun—Mercury, Venus, Earth, and Mars—are balls of solid or molten rock and metal. Each planet has a shallow atmosphere or no atmosphere at all, depending on its size and gravity, and only Earth has liquid water. These planets orbit the Sun in the same plane, but at different distances

The asteroid belt consists of countless rocky objects left over from the formation of the planets.

The Kuiper Belt is made of icy and rocky fragments left over from the formation of the solar system.

Comets are balls of ice and dust that swoop across the solar system, loop around the Sun, and then vanish beyond Neptune.

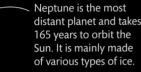

Neptune is the most distant planet and takes 165 years to orbit the Sun. It is mainly made of various types of ice.

Uranus is covered in blue-green clouds of methane and has a faint ring system like Saturn's. With temperatures as low as -371°F (-224°C), it is the coldest planet in the solar system.

DWARF PLANETS

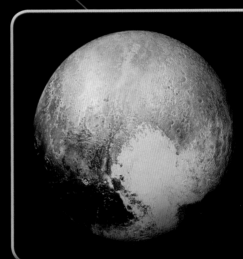

As well as the inner and outer planets, the solar system also contains at least five rocky dwarf planets, including Pluto. Unlike true planets, these share their orbits around the Sun with other objects such as asteroids. Pluto is basically a very large, spherical asteroid. It orbits the Sun in the Kuiper Belt beyond Neptune, alongside many smaller rocky or icy asteroids.

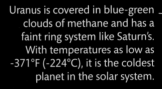

Jupiter's solid core is surrounded by swirling bands of colored gas that merge and turn into raging storms. Orbited by 67 moons, it is the biggest planet in the solar system.

Outer planets

Jupiter, Saturn, Uranus, and Neptune are gigantic balls of gas, liquid, and ice, with small rocky cores. They are far larger than the inner planets—the biggest, Jupiter, is more than 1,300 times the size of Earth. They are orbited by many moons, as well as smaller fragments of rock and ice such as those that form the rings of Saturn.

"The colossal **gravity** of Jupiter attracts many asteroids, shielding **Earth** from impacts that could destroy all life."

BLUE PLANET

Earth lies at the perfect distance from the Sun, allowing for an abundance of water to exist. If it were closer, the planet would be too hot and all the water would evaporate; if it were further away and colder, all the water would freeze. Liquid water forms the oceans, fuels the world's weather, and is vital for life. Without it, our planet would be a lifeless ball of rock.

LAYERED PLANET

Like the other planets of the solar system, Earth was created from the cloud of rock, dust, and gas that surrounded the newly formed Sun 4.6 billion years ago. This material welded together into a spherical mass of hot rock, which eventually melted and formed layers with a heavy metallic core. In time, planet Earth cooled and solidified, forming a rocky crust capped by oceans and an airy atmosphere.

CORE TO CRUST

Earth has a solid inner core of iron and nickel, and a metallic but liquid outer core. Surrounding the core is the deep mantle of hot but solid rock. The outermost rocky layer is the cool, brittle crust.

Earth is also known as the Blue Planet because of the abundance of liquid water on its surface.

Heat rising from the core keeps the hot mantle rock moving slowly, and fuels volcanic eruptions.

MOON

The Moon is made of the same rocks as Earth. It formed soon after Earth itself, from a cloud of rock and dust that surrounded Earth following the impact of one or more big asteroids.

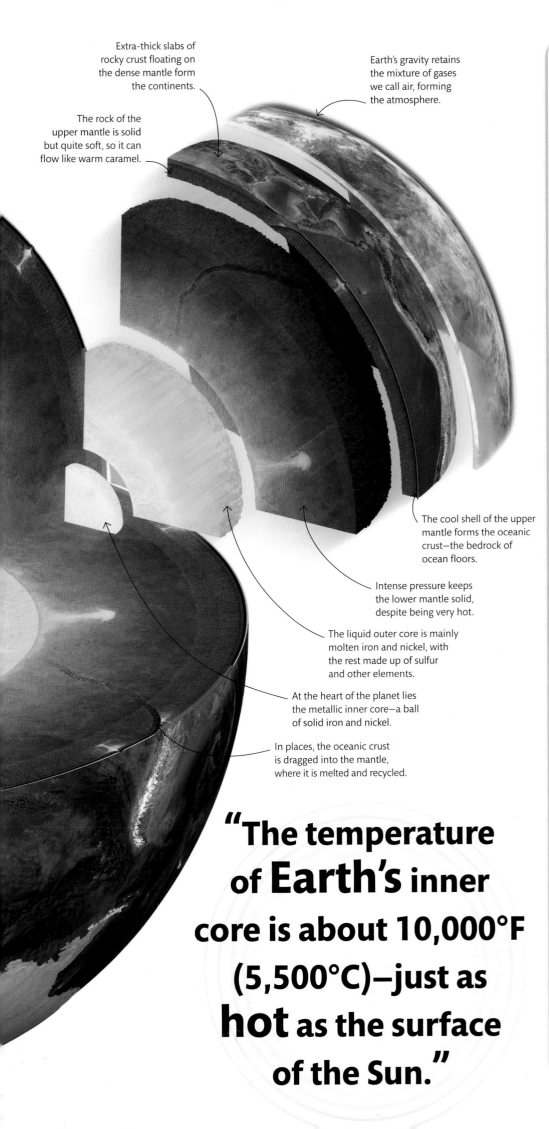

Extra-thick slabs of rocky crust floating on the dense mantle form the continents.

Earth's gravity retains the mixture of gases we call air, forming the atmosphere.

The rock of the upper mantle is solid but quite soft, so it can flow like warm caramel.

The cool shell of the upper mantle forms the oceanic crust—the bedrock of ocean floors.

Intense pressure keeps the lower mantle solid, despite being very hot.

The liquid outer core is mainly molten iron and nickel, with the rest made up of sulfur and other elements.

At the heart of the planet lies the metallic inner core—a ball of solid iron and nickel.

In places, the oceanic crust is dragged into the mantle, where it is melted and recycled.

"The temperature of **Earth's** inner core is about 10,000°F (5,500°C)—just as **hot** as the surface of the Sun."

EARLY EARTH

Earth was formed by the force of gravity, which makes objects floating in space attract each other. Gravity increases with mass, enabling a ball of dust to grow into a planet.

ACCRETION

As fragments of space rock collided due to gravity, the impact generated heat that partly melted these space rocks and welded them together. This process is called accretion.

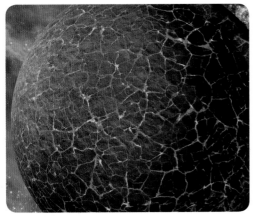

MELTDOWN

As Earth grew bigger, the heat built up by the impact of so much space rock made it melt. Most of the heavy iron sank to the center to form the planet's core.

AIR AND WATER

Massive volcanic eruptions during the planet's first 500 million years released water vapor and other gases, which formed the oceans and early atmosphere.

DYNAMIC EARTH

Earth's crust is constantly moving, driven by heat currents that originate deep within the planet. The movement is very slow, but immensely powerful. It has divided the crust into huge rocky plates that are pulling apart in some places and grinding together in others. The moving plates are slowly changing the global map.

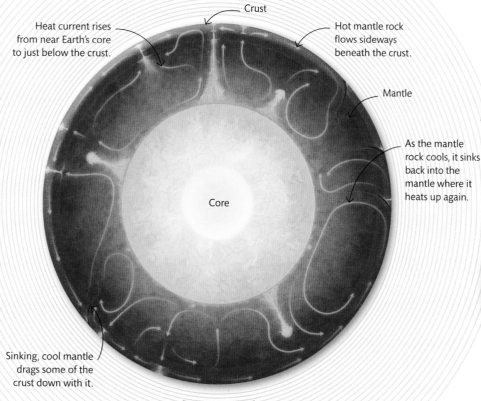

Crust

Heat current rises from near Earth's core to just below the crust.

Hot mantle rock flows sideways beneath the crust.

Mantle

As the mantle rock cools, it sinks back into the mantle where it heats up again.

Core

Sinking, cool mantle drags some of the crust down with it.

DEEP HEAT

Radioactive rock deep inside the planet releases energy, which generates heat in the same way as a nuclear reactor. The heat rises through the mantle to the surface in convection currents that circulate through the heat-softened mantle rock. The currents make the rock flow very slowly, so it rises to beneath the crust, spreads sideways, and sinks again as it cools.

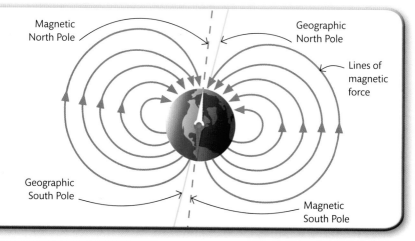

Most of the North American continent lies on the North American Plate.

The Pacific Plate is one of the biggest oceanic plates.

The East Pacific Rise is a spreading rift where new oceanic crust is being created.

Hotspots are areas of isolated volcanic activity.

KEY

▲ Volcanic zone

● Hotspot

● Earthquake zone

— Plate boundary

MAGNETIC FIELD

Earth's outer core is made of molten iron-rich metal. This is kept in motion by rising and sinking heat currents, and by the way the planet spins in space. The moving liquid metal generates electrical currents that create a magnetic field around Earth. This has a north and south pole, which are not quite aligned with Earth's geographic poles.

Magnetic North Pole

Geographic North Pole

Lines of magnetic force

Geographic South Pole

Magnetic South Pole

FRACTURED SHELL

The cool, brittle crust is broken into sections known as tectonic plates. Horizontal convection currents in the Earth's crust keep these plates constantly on the move. They are either pulling apart or pushing together, causing earthquakes and volcanoes. New crust is created where the plates are being pulled apart, and old crust is crumpled up or destroyed where the plates are colliding.

"Earth's crust moves at roughly the same speed as your fingernails grow."

FLOATING CONTINENTS

Earth's cool, brittle shell consists of thick continental crust and much thinner oceanic crust that forms the ocean floors. The rocks that form continents are lighter than ocean-floor rock, so they float on the dense mantle in the same way that ice floats on water. This is why the continents are higher than the ocean floors.

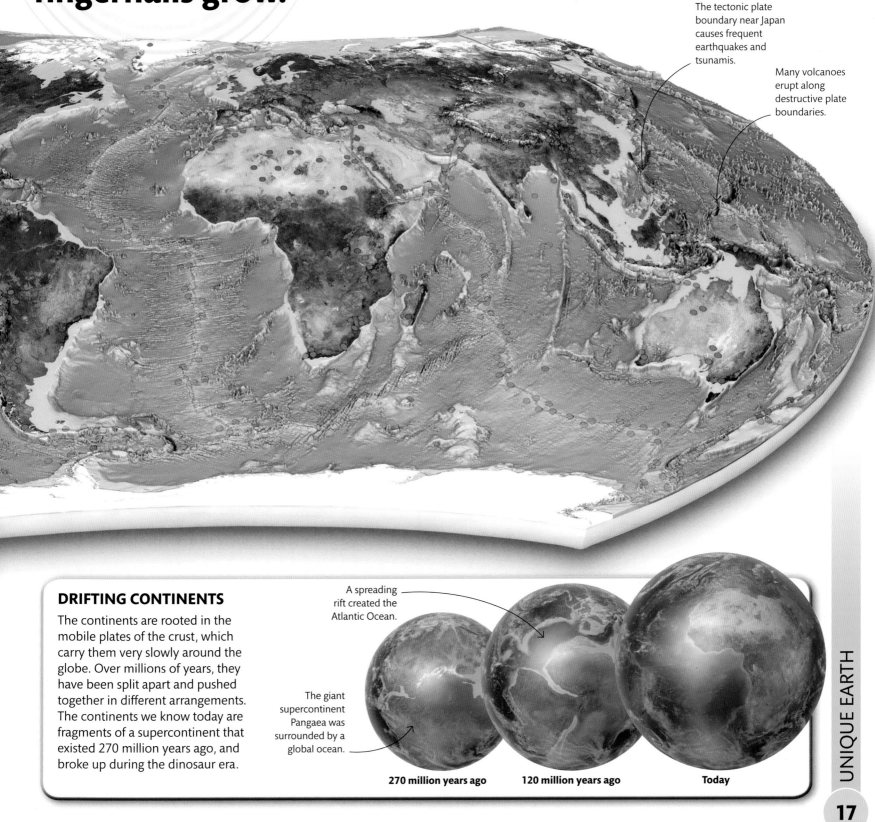

The tectonic plate boundary near Japan causes frequent earthquakes and tsunamis.

Many volcanoes erupt along destructive plate boundaries.

DRIFTING CONTINENTS

The continents are rooted in the mobile plates of the crust, which carry them very slowly around the globe. Over millions of years, they have been split apart and pushed together in different arrangements. The continents we know today are fragments of a supercontinent that existed 270 million years ago, and broke up during the dinosaur era.

A spreading rift created the Atlantic Ocean.

The giant supercontinent Pangaea was surrounded by a global ocean.

270 million years ago   **120 million years ago**   **Today**

SPREADING RIFTS

Where the moving plates of Earth's crust are pulling apart, they create spreading rifts that ease pressure on the hot rock below, allowing it to melt. The molten rock wells up into the rifts, where it forms new crust. Most of these rift zones are on the ocean floor, where the heat beneath pushes them up into ridges of submarine mountains. These mid-ocean ridges extend all around the planet, making them the longest mountain ranges on Earth.

MID-ATLANTIC RIDGE

The longest mid-ocean ridge runs from north to south along the floor of the Atlantic Ocean, and is up to 1.8 miles (3 km) high. The original rift began to form 200 million years ago, in the early Jurassic age of dinosaurs. It has been pulling apart at the rate of about 1 in (2.5 cm) per year ever since, dividing America from Europe and Africa.

TRANSFORM FAULTS

The rift of a mid-ocean ridge does not form a continuous line. It is frequently interrupted by huge fractures in the oceanic crust. These transform faults are caused by sections of ocean floor moving away from the rift in different directions. Where a fault offsets the rift, the rocks on each side of the fault slide past each other, causing earthquakes.

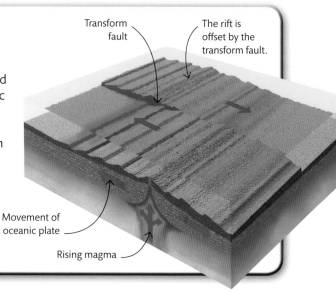

Transform fault

The rift is offset by the transform fault.

Movement of oceanic plate

Rising magma

North America

The ridge extends for about 9,900 miles (16,000 km)—from the Southern Ocean to the Arctic Ocean.

HYDROTHERMAL VENTS

The rift valley at the center of the ridge is dotted with hydrothermal vents—fountains of superheated water that erupt from the hot rock. Minerals dissolved from the rock by the very hot water turn to solid particles in the cold ocean, forming white smokers or sooty black smokers.

The central rift is flanked by transform faults caused by parts of the ocean floor moving in different ways.

South America

Thick continental crust forms the continent of South America.

Extraordinary animals such as these giant tubeworms form dense colonies around the vents.

Thin oceanic crust forms the ocean floor of the South Atlantic.

Ocean floor at the ridge is raised by the expansion of hot mantle rock below the crust.

ICELAND

In the far North Atlantic, a plume of heat rising through Earth's mantle has produced enough magma to raise part of the Mid-Atlantic Ridge above the waves. It forms Iceland, famous for its volcanoes and geysers. The whole island is made of basalt rock erupted from the spreading rift of the mid-ocean ridge—the same dark, heavy rock that forms the deep ocean floors.

EXPANDING OCEANS

As new oceanic crust is formed in a spreading rift, the ocean floor grows wider. In 180 million years this has made the Atlantic Ocean grow from a narrow valley to a broad ocean. The same process is in its early stages in the Red Sea, a spreading rift growing at about 0.4 in (1 cm) a year.

RED SEA
The Red Sea has formed where the Arabian and African plates are being pulled steadily apart. It will eventually become an ocean.

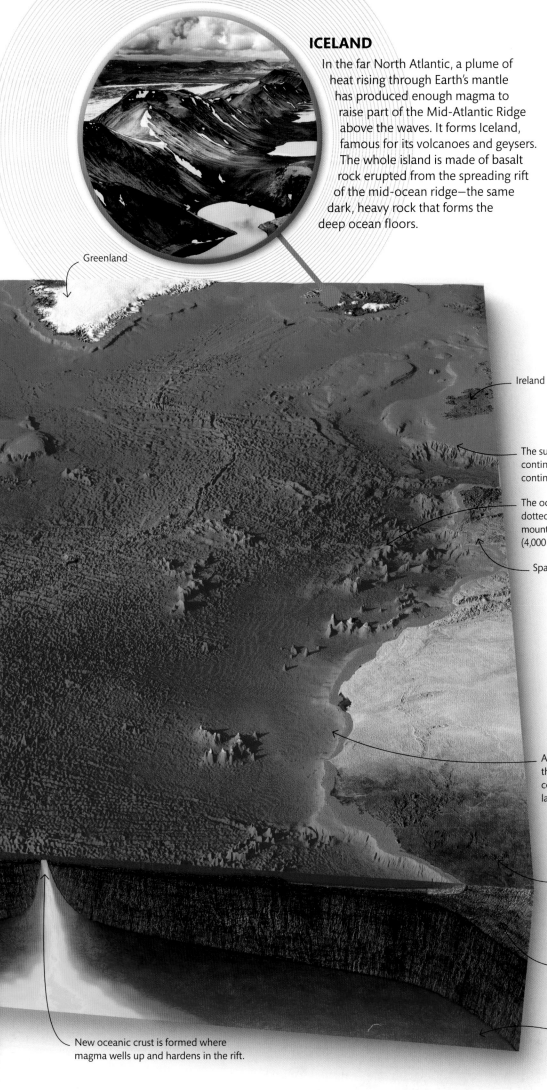

Greenland

Ireland

The submerged edge of a continent forms a shallow continental shelf.

The ocean floor is dotted with submarine mountains up to 13,000 ft (4,000 m) high.

Spain

Away from the ridge, the ocean floor is covered with deep layers of soft sediment.

Africa

Continental crust rock is lighter than mantle rock, so it floats on top of it.

The mantle rock is very hot but normally kept solid by pressure.

New oceanic crust is formed where magma wells up and hardens in the rift.

PILLOW LAVA

Molten rock erupting on the ocean floor hardens on the outside as soon as it hits the cold water. But internal pressure makes it burst through the hard shell to form a series of rounded lobes. When these finally solidify, they are called pillow lavas.

COLLISION ZONES

As new oceanic crust is created at plate boundaries that are pulling apart, old oceanic crust is destroyed at other boundaries where plates are pushing together. The edge of one plate dives beneath another in a process called subduction. This creates deep ocean trenches and chains of volcanic islands, pushes up mountain ranges, and causes earthquakes and tsunamis.

"Earth's crust is destroyed as fast as it is created."

OCEANIC DESTRUCTION

Where two plates of oceanic crust push together, the plate with the oldest, heaviest rock is forced below the other and destroyed. As it sinks it carries water and minerals with it. These are heated and rise through the upper plate, making some of the rock melt. The molten rock erupts from the ocean floor, forming lines of volcanoes called island arcs.

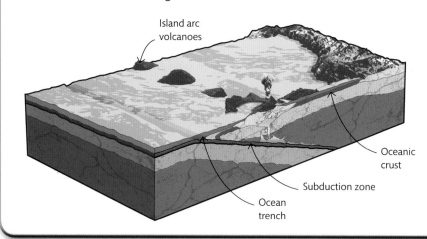

Island arc volcanoes

Oceanic crust

Subduction zone

Ocean trench

ALEUTIAN ISLAND ARC
This chain of 69 volcanic islands linking Alaska and Siberia marks where the Pacific Ocean floor is diving beneath the bed of the Bering Sea.

BUILDING MOUNTAINS

In places where oceanic crust collides with continental crust, the heavier oceanic rock pushes under the continent. The pressure of the colliding plates makes the edge of the continent crumple up, forming a range of fold mountains such as the South American Andes. Molten rock forming below the mountains erupts through chains of volcanoes.

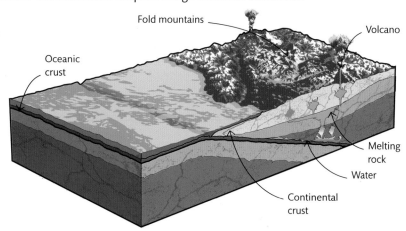

Fold mountains

Volcano

Oceanic crust

Melting rock

Water

Continental crust

MOUNT ST HELENS
The mountains and volcanoes of North America's Cascade Range were created by heavy oceanic crust grinding beneath the continent.

CRASHING CONTINENTS

Continental crust is made of relatively light rocks that float on Earth's heavy mantle like rafts. They cannot sink into it, so if two plates of continental crust collide, they both crumple at the edges to form high fold mountains. The Himalayas formed in this way. Deep below the mountains one slab of heavy upper mantle rock pushes beneath another, and this may lead to melting. But much of this molten rock stays below ground, where it eventually turns to solid granite.

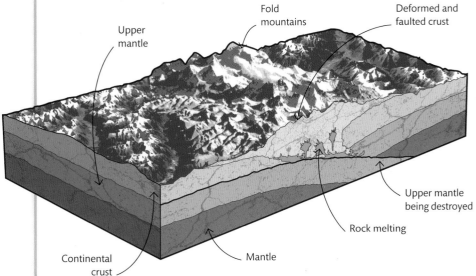

Upper mantle

Fold mountains

Deformed and faulted crust

Upper mantle being destroyed

Rock melting

Continental crust

Mantle

ALPS
Seventy million years ago, Italy collided with the rest of Europe, pushing up the Alps. This satellite view shows how they form a belt of crumpled, snow-capped fold mountains in the collision zone.

RING OF FIRE

Most of the world's subduction zones lie around the edge of the Pacific Ocean. They form a chain of deep ocean trenches, volcanoes, and mountains extending from the north of New Zealand to Alaska and down the Pacific coast of the Americas. They are so violently active that they are known as the Pacific Ring of Fire. More than 75 percent of the world's volcanoes have erupted here, and the Ring of Fire is also responsible for about 90 percent of the world's earthquakes.

An ocean trench forms where one plate of oceanic crust is slipping beneath another, or beneath a continent.

OCEAN TRENCHES

The places where oceanic crust is destroyed are marked by deep trenches in the ocean floor. On average, the oceans are 12,470 feet (3,800 m) deep, but some ocean trenches plunge to depths of 23,000 feet (7,000 m) or more. The deepest, the Mariana Trench in the western Pacific, is nearly 36,000 feet (11,000 m) below the waves.

GAPING SEAM

Iceland formed from rock that erupted from the Mid-Atlantic Ridge where it breaks the surface near Greenland. The rift between the North American and Eurasian plates passes right through the island, creating broad valleys. This is one of many ragged faults ripped in the floor of the Thingvellir rift valley where it is being slowly pulled apart.

EARTHQUAKES

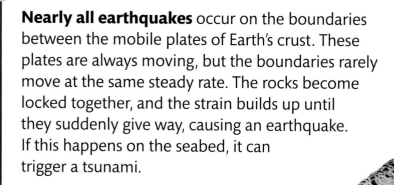

Nearly all earthquakes occur on the boundaries between the mobile plates of Earth's crust. These plates are always moving, but the boundaries rarely move at the same steady rate. The rocks become locked together, and the strain builds up until they suddenly give way, causing an earthquake. If this happens on the seabed, it can trigger a tsunami.

This plate of Earth's crust is moving very slowly, but its edge has locked against another plate.

SHOCK WAVE

When a boundary between moving plates keeps slipping, it causes minor tremors. But if the boundary is locked, the edges of the plates get distorted like bent springs. When the rocks give way, all the movement that should have occurred over many years happens within a few minutes, generating the shock wave we call an earthquake.

An earthquake is caused by a sudden movement of the fault line where the plates slide past each other.

The point where the fault has given way is the focus of the earthquake. It is deep under ground.

Most damage occurs directly above the focus. This is called the epicenter.

DESTRUCTIVE FORCE

Although most earthquakes last only a few minutes, they can be devastating. Some of the damage may be the result of movement of the rocks along a fault line. But most of the destruction is caused by the shock waves that travel out from the focus of the earthquake. These can shake the ground with such violence that anything built on it is certain to collapse.

STRUCTURAL COLLAPSE

Shaking ground makes brick or stone buildings crumble and collapse. Even steel-framed buildings can topple as the ground shifts beneath them.

LANDSLIDES

In hilly regions, rock and soil can be loosened by an earthquake and surge downhill in a landslide. If this hits a town, it can have devastating effects.

FIRES

Earthquakes that hit cities often fracture gas pipes, oil tanks, and electrical cables, causing fires. These can result in far more damage than the earthquake itself.

Shock waves spread out from the focus of the earthquake like ripples on a pond. They shake the ground, often causing great destruction.

INSIDE EARTH

The shock waves from an earthquake are detected all around the world by instruments called seismometers. The way these shock waves travel through the planet varies according to their nature and the layers they pass through. This has enabled scientists to work out the internal structure of our planet.

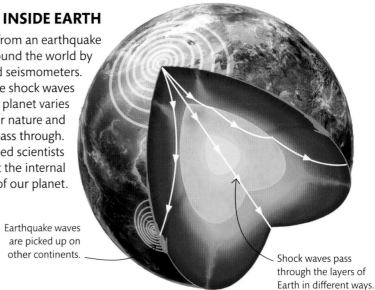

Earthquake waves are picked up on other continents.

Shock waves pass through the layers of Earth in different ways.

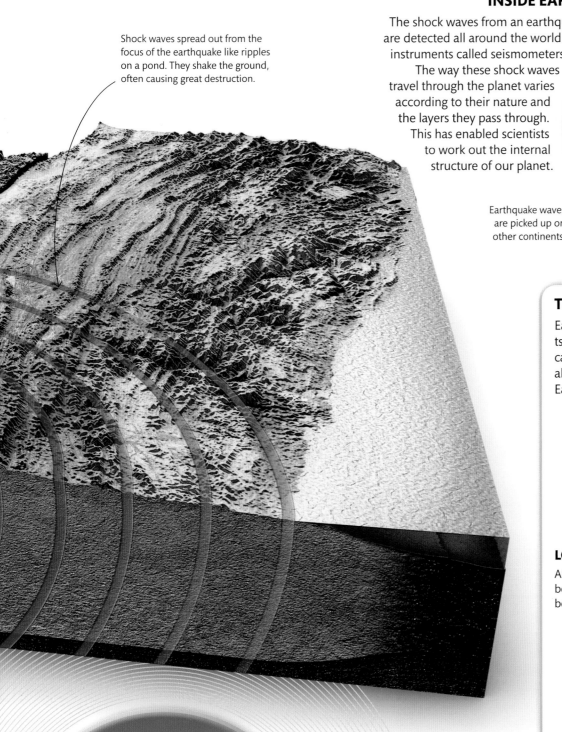

TSUNAMI

Earthquakes beneath the sea can trigger tsunamis. The most devastating have been caused by a sudden uplift of the ocean floor rocks above subduction zones, where one plate of Earth's crust is slipping beneath another.

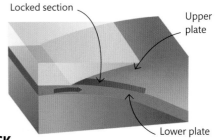

Locked section

Upper plate

Lower plate

LOCK

Although the lower plate may slide harmlessly beneath the upper plate, the two plates often become locked together.

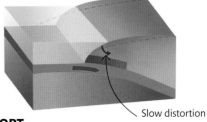

Slow distortion

DISTORT

As the lower plate keeps moving, it drags the locked section of the upper plate downward. This distorts the edge of the upper plate, building up tension.

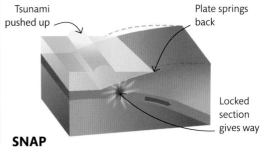

Tsunami pushed up

Plate springs back

Locked section gives way

SNAP

Eventually, the rocks give way. The edge of the upper plate margin springs upwards, pushing the water up into a giant heap that becomes a tsunami.

UPLIFT

An earthquake can make dramatic changes to the landscape. In 1964, a massive earthquake on the Pacific coast of Alaska lifted this shipwreck right out of the sea, so it now sits stranded on an island. It was lifted nearly 16 ft (5 m) in less than five minutes. Other parts of Alaska sank by 8 ft (2.4 m).

VOLCANOES

Most volcanoes mark the boundaries between the moving plates of Earth's crust. Some erupt through spreading rifts where plates are moving apart; others erupt over subduction zones where plates are grinding together. There are also hotspot volcanoes, fueled by isolated heat currents rising beneath the crust.

ERUPTION TYPES

Volcanoes erupt in different ways depending on their geological location. Oceanic volcanoes erupt liquid lava made of melted mantle rock that flows easily. Continental volcanoes produce sticky lava that can block volcanic vents, leading to explosive eruptions. There are also many varieties in between.

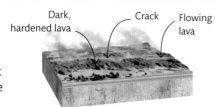

Dark, hardened lava — Crack — Flowing lava

Fissure

In this type of eruption, spreading rifts may create long cracks that erupt liquid basalt lava. These occur mainly on the ocean floors, but can also be seen in Iceland.

Fire fountain erupts into the air.

Side vent — Lava spills out from the crater.

Either a small or no ash cloud. — Lava bombs are hurled into the air.

Hawaiian

Oceanic hotspot volcanoes erupt liquid lava that flows quickly but quietly downhill from the crater. They may also produce fire fountains of lava.

Strombolian

In a Strombolian eruption, the lava is stickier and contains more gas. The gas expands rapidly when it reaches the crater, blasting molten lava high into the sky.

Medium-height ash plume

Volcanic bombs

Vulcanian

When lava contains a lot of silica—the mineral used to make glass—it is so sticky that it often solidifies in the vent. This makes pressure build up, causing rare but violent eruptions.

Towering ash cloud

Rain of ash

Lava

Plinian

The largest and most explosive eruptions blast lava and ash high into the air. The ash cloud may collapse and surge downhill in a deadly cascade.

FIRE MOUNTAINS

A typical volcano is a tall cone topped by a crater that erupts lava and volcanic ash. These settle around the crater to build up the cone. But some volcanoes are very different, and may be hard to recognize.

Stratovolcano

This type of volcano forms where one of Earth's plates is slipping beneath another. It releases sticky lava that does not flow far, and layers of lava and ash form a steep cone.

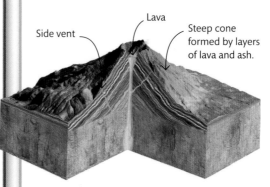

Side vent — Lava — Steep cone formed by layers of lava and ash.

ARENAL VOLCANO
Glowing lava tumbles down the flank of Arenal, a stratovolcano in Costa Rica.

Shield volcano

Volcanoes that erupt from spreading rifts or oceanic hotspots produce very fluid lava. This lava can flow a long way before cooling enough to turn solid, forming a broad shield volcano.

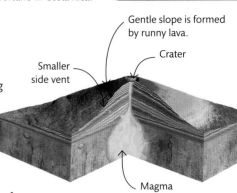

Gentle slope is formed by runny lava.

Crater

Smaller side vent

Magma

PITON DE LA FOURNAISE
This shield volcano on Réunion island in the Pacific Ocean is one of the most active volcanoes in the world.

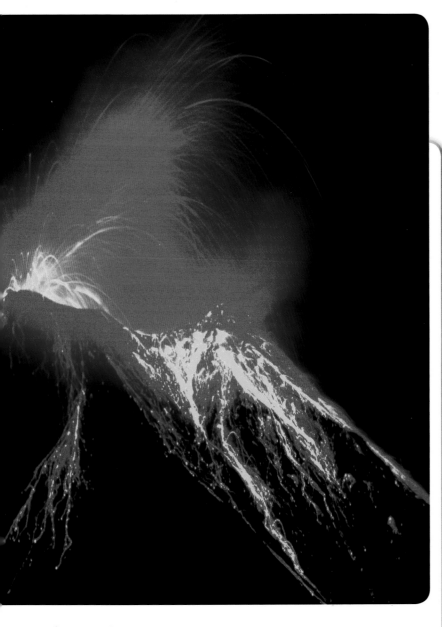

CALDERAS

A volcano that does not erupt for centuries often has a blocked crater. It builds up pressure below the blockage until it blows it into the sky in a massive eruption. This empties the magma chamber inside the volcano, so its unsupported peak collapses into the empty space. The result is a broad caldera that is much wider than the original crater.

MOUNT ST HELENS
This stratovolcano in the USA used to have a cone-shaped peak. But in May 1980 a catastrophic eruption made the top of the volcano cave in, forming a caldera. A new volcanic cone is growing inside the caldera.

SUPERVOLCANOES

The biggest, most dangerous volcanoes erupt with such shattering force that all the debris is blown far away. This means that there is no cone, and the only clear evidence may be a huge caldera that forms a water-filled lake, often dotted with hot springs. The eruptions of such supervolcanoes in the past have devastated life on Earth.

TOBA SUPERVOLCANO
Lake Toba in Indonesia is a gigantic caldera created by the biggest known volcanic eruption in the last 2 million years. Its central island has been pushed up by magma pressure.

Fissure volcano

In rift zones, liquid lava may well up from a fissure in the crust and flow away in a flood of molten rock. When the lava hardens, it forms a flat sheet called a flood basalt.

Erupting lava

Flood basalt

Fissure in crust

HOLUHRAUN
The ribbon of fiery lava erupting from this Icelandic fissure created a lava field covering 33 sq miles (85 sq km).

SUPERHEATED WATER

Volcanoes are the most dramatic features of Earth's tectonic plate boundaries and hotspots. But molten rock rising through the crust can also heat water that has seeped into the ground. Since hot water tends to rise, it finds its way back to the surface, where it erupts as hot springs, geysers, and other geothermal features. Unlike most volcanoes, they are often constantly active.

HIGH PRESSURE

All geothermal features are caused by water being heated deep below ground. The high pressure at depth enables the water to be superheated to well above its normal boiling point. This makes it dissolve minerals from the rocks. The hot, mineral-rich water rises through vents, often forming hot springs or escaping as steam at fumaroles. Pressure building up in the vents can power spectacular geysers. Chemicals in the water may also attack the rock and turn it to hot liquid mud that bubbles up as mudpots.

This geyser erupts at frequent, regular intervals, exploding from a vent in the floor of a shallow pool.

Water often turns to steam before it reaches the surface, and erupts from a fumarole.

When some of the hot water in this chamber escapes, pressure drops. This allows water below to boil and erupt as a geyser.

The weight of hot water in the chamber above makes pressure build up in this vent, heating water to above normal boiling point.

Volcanic sulfur gas dissolved in water creates sulfuric acid. This turns porous rock to mud, which bubbles from a mudpot.

Magma deep below ground heats this rock, and the water in the porous rock above it.

GEOTHERMAL FIELDS

Most hot springs, geysers, and similar features occur where the plates of Earth's crust are pulling apart. They include these fumaroles in Iceland, as well as the black smokers that erupt from mid-ocean ridges. But some of the most famous are fueled by the heat of dormant supervolcanoes such as Yellowstone in the US. All these features are often grouped together in clusters called geothermal fields.

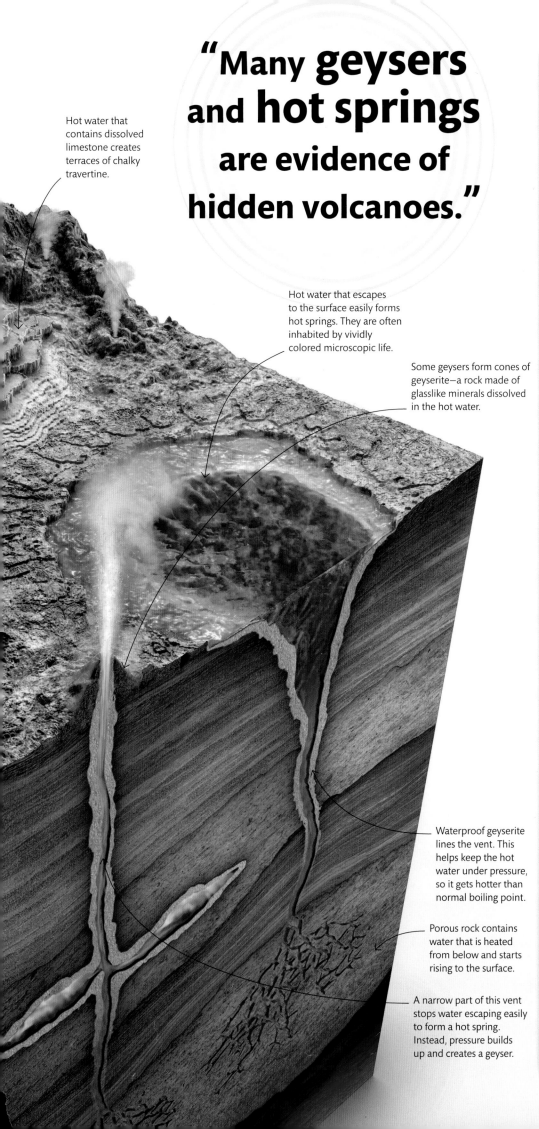

"Many geysers and hot springs are evidence of hidden volcanoes."

Hot water that contains dissolved limestone creates terraces of chalky travertine.

Hot water that escapes to the surface easily forms hot springs. They are often inhabited by vividly colored microscopic life.

Some geysers form cones of geyserite—a rock made of glasslike minerals dissolved in the hot water.

Waterproof geyserite lines the vent. This helps keep the hot water under pressure, so it gets hotter than normal boiling point.

Porous rock contains water that is heated from below and starts rising to the surface.

A narrow part of this vent stops water escaping easily to form a hot spring. Instead, pressure builds up and creates a geyser.

AROUND THE WORLD

WARM WATER
In the mountains of central Japan, monkeys called Japanese macaques bathe in the pools of hot springs to keep warm in winter. Some hot springs are used by people too, but many are far too hot for this.

GIANT GEYSER
Steamboat Geyser in Yellowstone National Park is the world's largest active geyser. A major eruption can hurl hot water more than 295 ft (90 m) into the air, but such eruptions do not happen very often.

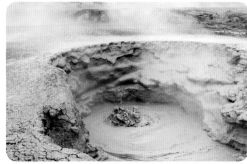

BUBBLING MUD
On the volcanic island of Iceland, acidic hot springs seeping up through volcanic ash have created bubbling pools of liquid mud. The bubbles are full of gas, and burst with a sulfurous smell of rotten eggs.

VOLCANIC STEAM
This fumarole on the Mediterranean island of Vulcano erupts steam containing dissolved sulfur. As the steam is cooled by the air, the sulfur turns to bright yellow crystals that cover the volcanic rock around the vent.

UNDER PRESSURE

As Strokkur geyser in Iceland begins to erupt, steam pressure below ground pushes hot water up into a glittering blue dome. Within seconds, the dome explodes in a fountain of water and steam up to 100 ft (30 m) high. Active every six to ten minutes, Strokkur is one of more than 50 geothermal features in Iceland's Haukadalur rift valley.

ROCKY PLANET

Earth's crust is made of many types of rock. Some are created from cooling molten lava or magma, while others are made of rock fragments that have been cemented together. Intense heat and pressure can change one type of rock to another. Meanwhile, the processes of weathering and erosion are continually breaking up solid rock, creating the soft sediments that form new rock.

THE ROCK CYCLE

Molten rock that erupts from deep below the ground is worn away when it is exposed to the weather. It is turned to sand and clay, which are often swept into the sea. Here they settle in layers that gradually harden, forming sedimentary rock. When buried deep underground, these rocks can be turned into harder rocks by the intense heat and pressure.

FAULTING AND FOLDING

Where the mobile plates of Earth's crust collide, rock layers are squeezed and folded by the pressure. They can be turned on end or even upside down. The rocks can also fracture, so the layers slip out of alignment along fault lines. The largest faults form boundaries between the mobile plates, and their movement causes earthquakes.

Lava erupts from volcanoes and cools to form volcanic igneous rocks.

Glacier ice reduces rock to rubble, and grinds some of it to powder.

Rocks attacked by ice, rain, and heat crumble and form the soil in which plants grow.

Some magma erupts from volcanoes as lava and ash, which create volcanic cones.

Magma often turns solid below ground to form igneous rocks like granite.

Chemical changes make hot rock melt and form magma that seeps upwards.

Heat and pressure transform sedimentary rocks into harder metamorphic rocks.

Squeezed and folded by massive forces, rocks are pushed up into mountain ranges.

Sedimentary rock buried deep in the crust is compressed and heated, changing its nature.

The moving plates of Earth's crust drag layers of rock beneath continents.

FOSSILS

Some sedimentary rocks contain the remains of living things that died long ago. Most of these fossils preserve bones or shells that allow scientists to trace the evolution of life. They are also useful for dating rocks, since any rocks that contain the same fossils must have been formed at the same time.

Rain is slightly acidic in nature, and dissolves some of the minerals that hold rocks together.

Rivers carve valleys through the landscape, turning rock to smaller and smaller particles.

Sand, silt, and clay particles carried by flowing river water are swept into the sea and carried far offshore.

Skeletons of microscopic sea life settle on the seabed and build up deep layers.

Soft sediments on the seabed are gradually buried and compacted.

Compacted sediments eventually turn to hard sedimentary rock.

ROCK TYPES

There are hundreds of different types of rock, but they can be grouped into three main types—igneous, sedimentary, and metamorphic. Each type of rock can be turned into another by the processes involved in the rock cycle.

GRANITE

BASALT

Basalt is the most common igneous rock on the planet. It forms much of Earth's ocean floor.

IGNEOUS ROCK

When molten magma or lava cools and turns solid, it creates igneous rocks such as granite or basalt. These are made of interlocking crystals, making them very hard. They form large masses instead of layers.

SANDSTONE

Sandstone varies in colour from white to yellow and red.

LIMESTONE

SEDIMENTARY ROCK

Over millions of years, soft sediments like sand or mud are cemented together by dissolved minerals, creating sedimentary rocks. They can be hard or soft, but always form layers that may be folded by Earth's forces.

MARBLE

SCHIST

METAMORPHIC ROCK

Heat and pressure can change a rock's nature in a process called metamorphism. A soft sedimentary rock may be transformed to hard schist, which still shows its original layers, while baked limestone turns to marble.

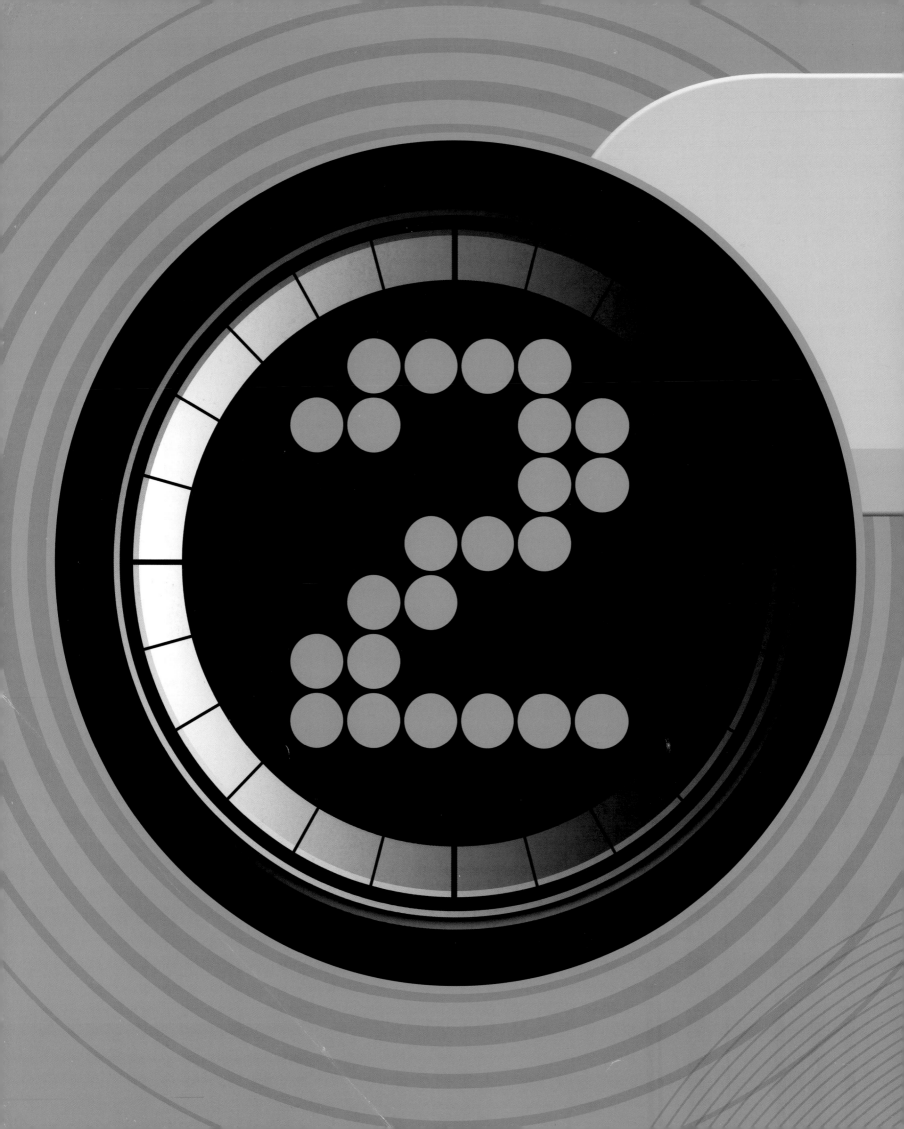

FORMIDABLE FORMATIONS

Earth is in a constant state of transformation as titanic forces within the planet raise mountains and the relentless power of the weather slowly grinds them down again. This endless process of mountain building and erosion has created some of the world's most magnificent landscapes.

TITANIC FORCES
ANDES MOUNTAIN RANGE

Nowhere on Earth are the titanic forces that build mountains more evident than in the Andes. Extending the length of South America, this long chain of rugged peaks has been forced up by the Pacific Ocean floor pushing beneath the edge of the continent. Buckled and fractured by the relentless pressure, vast slabs of continental rock have been thrust upward, while the process has fueled the eruption of countless volcanoes.

Making mountains

Part of the Pacific Ocean floor is moving northeast at about 2 in (5 cm) a year, forcing a slab of heavy oceanic crust beneath South America. Meanwhile, the continent is moving westward at about 1.2 in (3 cm) a year. The pressure has created giant faults that act like wedges driven beneath the central Andes, squeezing them upward.

Dotted with volcanoes, the Andes are one of the world's highest and most spectacular mountain ranges.

The point where the ocean floor plunges beneath the continent is marked by the deep Peru-Chile Trench.

Most of the Andes range is being pushed up by the Nazca Plate, which forms the floor of the southeastern Pacific Ocean.

AT A GLANCE

- **LOCATION** Western side of South America
- **EXTENT** 4,500 miles (7,200 km)
- **AGE** More than 25 million years old
- **ORIGIN** Oceanic-continental subduction

STATS AND FACTS

The South American Andes include the world's highest mountains outside Asia, and they form the longest range of mountains on any continent. They also include the world's highest volcanoes.

HIGHEST MOUNTAIN

Aconcagua in Argentina is the highest Andean mountain at 22,838 ft (6,961 m).

RISING PEAKS

The mountains have nearly doubled their height in the last 10 million years.

HIGH PLATEAU

The air in the Altiplano plateau contains only half as much oxygen as the air at sea level.

VOLCANOES

With 183 active volcanoes, the Andes is one of Earth's most volcanic mountain belts.

Ocean floor grinding beneath the continent contains seawater that has seeped into the rock.

The coastal block of the continent is being pushed eastward by the moving slab of oceanic crust.

LONGEST MOUNTAIN CHAIN ON LAND

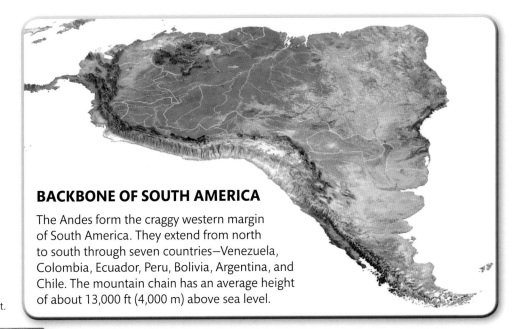

BACKBONE OF SOUTH AMERICA

The Andes form the craggy western margin of South America. They extend from north to south through seven countries—Venezuela, Colombia, Ecuador, Peru, Bolivia, Argentina, and Chile. The mountain chain has an average height of about 13,000 ft (4,000 m) above sea level.

Lake Titicaca at the northern end of the Altiplano plateau is the highest navigable lake in the world.

The Altiplano plateau, lying 12,300 ft (3,750 m) above sea level, has been raised high above the rest of the continent.

The dry climate of the high Andes has created the Salar de Uyuni—the world's largest salt flat.

Movement along the deep thrust fault has fractured and crumpled the rocks above, forming ranges of fold mountains.

Westward movement of the South American Plate has created a huge thrust fault beneath the eastern Andes.

The South American Plate is creeping west, driven by the spreading Mid-Atlantic Ridge.

As the descending slab is heated by the hot mantle, water boils out of it and seeps into the hot rock above.

The water makes the hot rock melt, forming magma that rises through faults and erupts from volcanoes.

Squeezed between two moving plates, a huge block of continental crust is forced upward.

ANDEAN PEAKS

The Andes are at their most dramatic in southern Chile, where the jagged spines of the Torres del Paine soar straight up into the sky. These granite peaks originally welled up as molten magma within the fold mountains. The surrounding rock has been scoured away by glacier ice to leave the much harder, more resistant granite core.

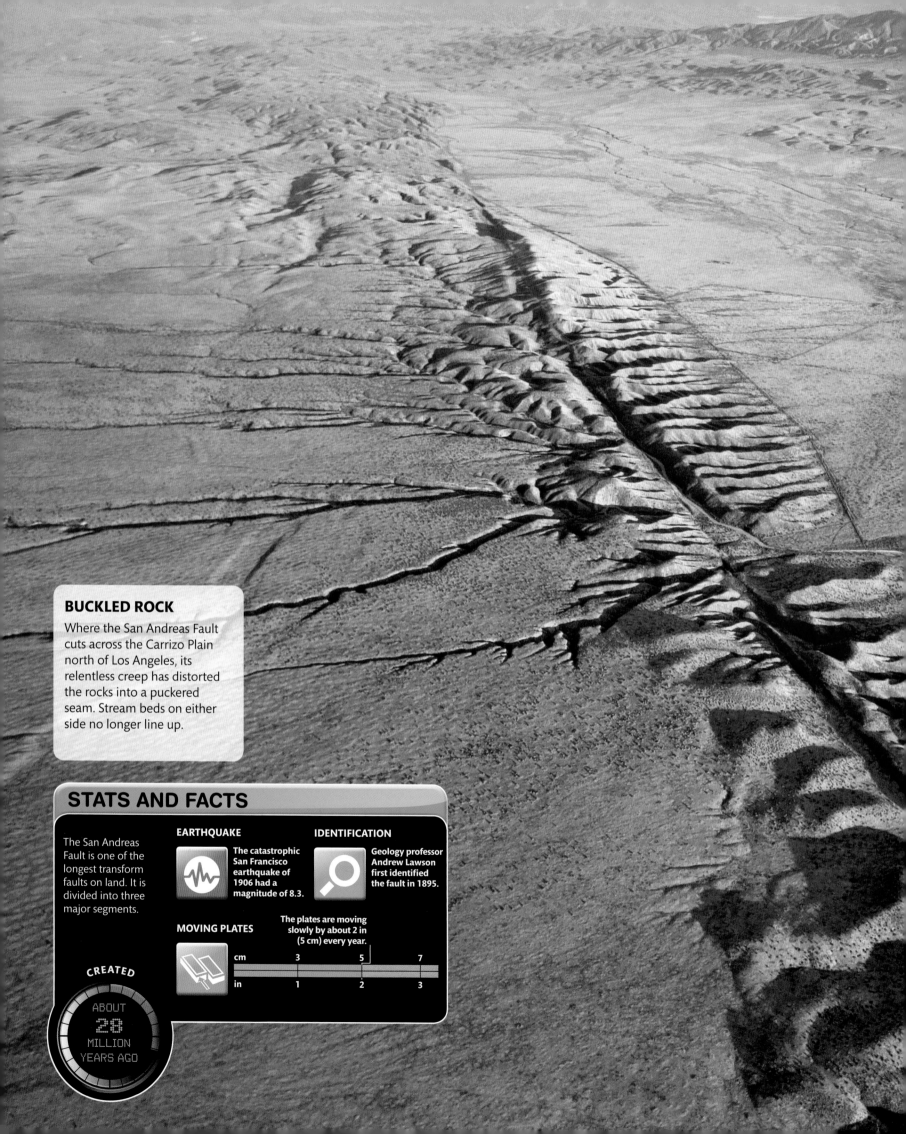

BUCKLED ROCK

Where the San Andreas Fault cuts across the Carrizo Plain north of Los Angeles, its relentless creep has distorted the rocks into a puckered seam. Stream beds on either side no longer line up.

STATS AND FACTS

The San Andreas Fault is one of the longest transform faults on land. It is divided into three major segments.

EARTHQUAKE

The catastrophic San Francisco earthquake of 1906 had a magnitude of 8.3.

IDENTIFICATION

Geology professor Andrew Lawson first identified the fault in 1895.

MOVING PLATES

The plates are moving slowly by about 2 in (5 cm) every year.

cm		3		5		7
in	1		2		3	

CREATED

ABOUT
28
MILLION
YEARS AGO

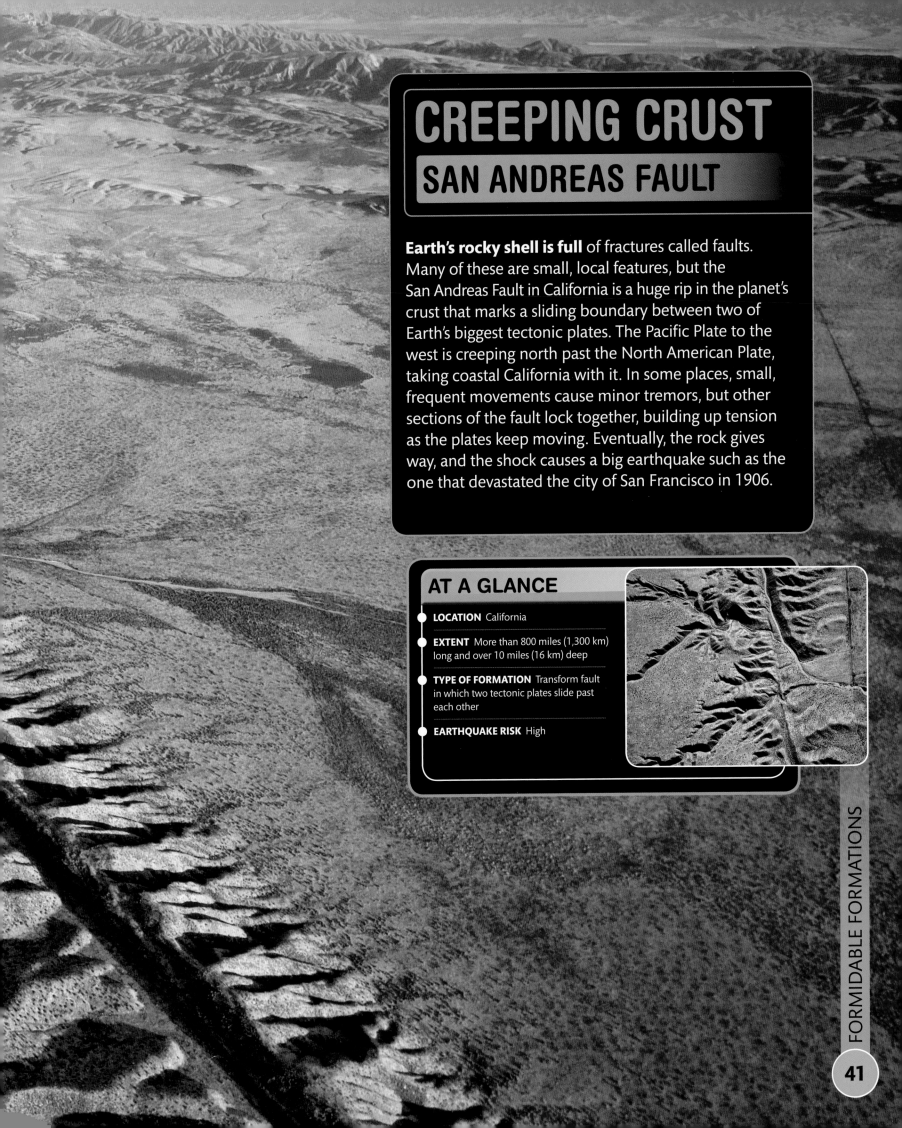

CREEPING CRUST
SAN ANDREAS FAULT

Earth's rocky shell is full of fractures called faults. Many of these are small, local features, but the San Andreas Fault in California is a huge rip in the planet's crust that marks a sliding boundary between two of Earth's biggest tectonic plates. The Pacific Plate to the west is creeping north past the North American Plate, taking coastal California with it. In some places, small, frequent movements cause minor tremors, but other sections of the fault lock together, building up tension as the plates keep moving. Eventually, the rock gives way, and the shock causes a big earthquake such as the one that devastated the city of San Francisco in 1906.

AT A GLANCE

- **LOCATION** California

- **EXTENT** More than 800 miles (1,300 km) long and over 10 miles (16 km) deep

- **TYPE OF FORMATION** Transform fault in which two tectonic plates slide past each other

- **EARTHQUAKE RISK** High

SACRED MOUNTAIN
ULURU

Lying at the very heart of Australia, Uluru rises like an island above a vast expanse of desert sand, forming the continent's most famous natural landmark. It is the exposed end of a layered bed of sandstone which has been bent upright by the titanic forces that build mountains. Most of Uluru's immense bulk lies below ground. The rock is very hard, but it has been eroded into rounded forms by desert storms that send water cascading down its gullies to the plain below.

AT A GLANCE

- **LOCATION** Central Australia

- **HEIGHT** 1,142 ft (348 m) above the surrounding ground level

- **FORMATION** An inselberg (island mountain) eroded by flash floods

- **AGE** The sandstone of Uluru is more than 530 million years old

STATS AND FACTS

Also known as Ayers Rock, Uluru is sacred to the local native people. Some caves in the sandstone contain ancient rock paintings.

HUMAN PRESENCE

Findings show that humans settled in the area more than 10,000 years ago.

THICKNESS

The exposed sandstone beds have a thickness of at least 7,900 ft (2,400 m).

TEMPERATURE

Daytime temperatures of 115°F (46°C) have been recorded during summer.

°C   15   30   45   60
°F   50   100

CIRCUMFERENCE

5.8 MILES (9.4 KM)

"The sandstone beds were probably tilted upright more than 300 million years ago."

RED ROCK

Iron compounds in Uluru's sandstone turn to rusty iron oxide at the surface, giving it a red glow at sunrise and sunset. At other times, it may look pink or even violet.

THE ROOF OF THE WORLD

MOUNT EVEREST

Sixty million years ago, India was an island continent that was being dragged north by the mobile plates of Earth's crust. About 10 million years later, it slammed into Asia, and this collision pushed up an immense mountain range, the Himalayas, and the neighboring Tibetan Plateau. The whole region has been called the "Roof of the World." The mountains here are the highest on Earth, and the highest of them all is Mount Everest. Its peak is so far above sea level that the air contains very little oxygen, and those mountaineers who try to climb it are forced to carry their own oxygen supplies.

AT A GLANCE

- **LOCATION** Border of Nepal and Tibet Autonomous Region, China

- **MOUNTAIN RANGE** Himalayas

- **SUMMIT HEIGHT** 29,029 ft (8,848 m) above sea level

- **AGE** Less than 50 million years

STATS AND FACTS

The subcontinent of India is still moving north and pushing up the Himalayas. As a result, they are still rising at the rate of about 0.2 in (5 mm) a year.

THE HIGHEST

Everest is one of 14 peaks on Earth that are more than 26,247 ft (8,000 m) high.

ICY BLAST

Wind speeds of up to 175 mph (280 km/h) have been recorded on the summit.

TEMPERATURE

Temperature at the summit can fall to -80°F (-62°C).

	°C	-62	-31	0
	°F	-80	-22	32

FIRST SUCCESSFUL CLIMB
1953

"All of the highest mountains on Earth are in the Himalayas and neighboring Karakoram range."

RED GIANTS

At Sossusvlei in the southern part of the Namib Desert, a dry clay pan called a vlei is surrounded by giant red sand dunes that are among the highest in the world. They are continually reshaped by the wind from all directions, and so are known as star dunes.

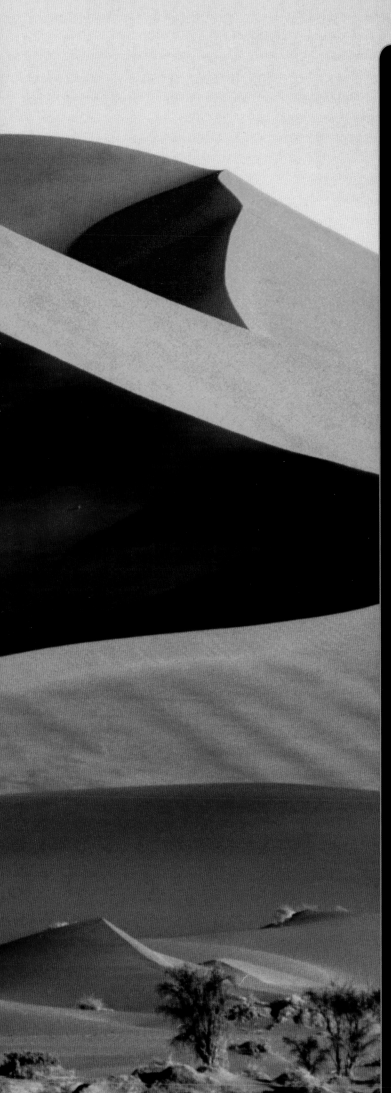

MOUNTAINS OF SAND
NAMIB DESERT DUNES

Dry desert sand is easily moved by the wind, which bounces it along over the ground and heaps it into sand dunes. In Africa's Namib Desert, winds coming from the nearby Atlantic have built up some of the highest and oldest dunes on Earth. Like all sand dunes, they are shaped by wind carrying sand up the windward face of each dune and making it fall over the crest to the sheltered side. This makes some dunes creep slowly downwind, while others have become fixed in place.

AT A GLANCE

- **LOCATION** Namibia, southwest Africa
- **LANDFORM** Desert sand dunes
- **FORMATION** Built up from wind-blown desert sand
- **AGE** The desert dunes have existed for at least 2 million years

STATS AND FACTS

Some of the biggest sand dunes in the world are found in the Sossusvlei region of the Namib Desert.

NAMIB DESERT

The desert itself has existed for at least 55 million years, making it the oldest desert on Earth.

RECORD BREAKER

At 1,273 ft (388 m) high, Dune 7 at Walvis Bay is the highest sand dune in the Namib Desert.

TEMPERATURE

Summer daytime temperatures can reach 113°F (45°C); at night they can dip to near freezing.

°C	10	20	30	40	50
°F	50	68	86	104	122

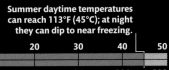

SPECTACULAR SIX-SIDED STONES
GIANT'S CAUSEWAY

Sixty million years ago, powerful forces dragging North America away from Europe opened a rift in Earth's crust on the western fringes of what is now Britain. The rift erupted floods of molten basalt—the rock that forms the ocean floors. As the basalt cooled and solidified, it started to shrink, splitting into thousands of regular geometric columns. Now worn away by the pounding waves of the Atlantic Ocean, they form a staircase of stepping stones leading down to the sea and beyond.

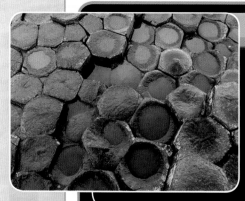

AT A GLANCE

- **LOCATION** Northeast coast of Northern Ireland
- **EXTENT** About ½ mile (1 km)
- **FORMATION** Cooling of basaltic lava flow from a volcanic eruption
- **AGE** About 60 million years old

STATS AND FACTS

The Giant's Causeway is a packed cluster of more than 40,000 interlocking columns. These have formed from many separate lava flows, stacked one on top of the other.

COLUMN SHAPES

Most columns have six sides but others have four, five, seven, or even eight sides.

FORMATIONS

Some formations have names such as Wishing Chair and Shepherd's Steps.

LAVA

The solidified lava flow is up to 92 ft (28 m) thick.

m	10	20	30	40
ft	50		100	

COLUMN HEIGHT

UP TO
39
FEET
(12 M)

GIANT STEPS

This remarkable geological feature starts at the foot of a sea cliff before disappearing below the waves. According to an Irish legend, the giant Finn MacCool built the causeway across the Irish Sea to reach Scotland, so he could fight a rival giant.

MULTICOLORED LAYERS
GRAND CANYON

One of the deepest river gorges in the world, the Grand Canyon in the USA was created by the colossal forces that build mountains. Over millions of years, they pushed up the rocks that form the Colorado Plateau, forcing the Colorado River to cut down through them. The result is a spectacular canyon, displaying dramatic layers of rock.

Natural wonder

The main canyon of the Colorado River is joined by side canyons cut by smaller streams, forming a complex pattern. Scorching summer heat and winter frost make the rock walls flake and crumble, so the canyon slowly grows wider.

GRAND CANYON REVEALED

Layers of sand, mud, and other sediments mainly laid down on the floor of a vanished ocean have turned to beds of solid sedimentary rock. The oldest lie at the bottom, above a layer of ancient rock that was tilted, faulted, and worn flat before the horizontal layers were deposited.

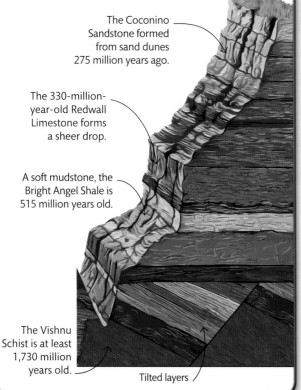

The Coconino Sandstone formed from sand dunes 275 million years ago.

The 330-million-year-old Redwall Limestone forms a sheer drop.

A soft mudstone, the Bright Angel Shale is 515 million years old.

The Vishnu Schist is at least 1,730 million years old.

Tilted layers

The South Rim of the canyon is 984 ft (300 m) lower than the North Rim.

Heavy rain in summer feeds streams that flow down the side canyons to join the river.

One of the oldest layers, the Vishnu Schist was formed by heat and pressure altering ancient sedimentary rock.

AT A GLANCE

- **LOCATION** Arizona, USA
- **LENGTH** 277 miles (446 km)
- **AVERAGE DEPTH** 1 mile (1.6 km)
- **AGE** About 20 million years

STATS AND FACTS

The exposed layers of rocks that form the high walls of the Grand Canyon provide Earth scientists with one of the most complete records of rock formation on the planet.

TEMPERATURE

On the South Rim, the temperature ranges from -4°F (-29°C) to 105°F (41°C).

RIVER EROSION

It takes about ten years for the river to widen the canyon by just a millimeter.

ROCK LAYERS

There are about 22 major rock layers; in parts, there can be as many as 40.

CANYON WIDTH

The widest part of the canyon is about 18 miles (29 km) across; the narrowest part is 3.7 miles (6 km).

HIDDEN IN THE LAYERS

Fossils of extinct sea creatures in the rocks show that most of the layers were laid down on the seabed. This trilobite was found in the Bright Angel Shale layer.

The youngest layer of rock is the pale Kaibab Limestone that forms the canyon rim.

The colder North Rim is more deeply eroded than the South Rim.

Molten rock erupting 1,700 million years ago cooled to form the Zoroaster Granite.

A fracture in the rock—a fault—has allowed the rock layers to move out of line.

The deepest rock layers lie at an angle because they were tilted by the collision of two plates of Earth's crust.

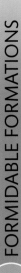

FORMIDABLE FORMATIONS

51

HORSESHOE BEND

The Grand Canyon has been carved out of the rocks of Arizona by the Colorado River as it flows west toward the Gulf of California in the US. Near the beginning of the canyon, a looping meander created early in the river's history has been etched deep into the desert landscape. The river now lies 1,000 ft (300 m) below the rim of the canyon.

SEA OF SALT
SALAR DE UYUNI

Covering an area ten times the size of the city of Los Angeles in the US, Salar de Uyuni is a vast expanse of gleaming crystalline salt. It was created by the evaporation of an ancient salt lake in the dry climate of the Bolivian Andes. As the water turned to vapor it left the salt behind, along with other minerals and elements such as the rare metal lithium. The result is the largest salt flat on Earth. Its surface is dotted with a few rocky islands—the peaks of ancient volcanoes that were once submerged by the lake, and now rise above a sea of salt.

AT A GLANCE

- **LOCATION** Bolivia, South America
- **ALTITUDE** 11,995 ft (3,656 m) above sea level
- **SIZE** 4,086 sq miles (10,582 sq km)
- **FORMATION** Made of salt crystals formed by evaporation of a salt lake

DAZZLING DECEPTION

Each year, heavy rain makes nearby lakes overflow and flood the salt flat with a shallow film of water. This creates such perfect reflections that the broad salt flat seems to become part of the sky.

FLATTEST
PLACE ON EARTH

STATS AND FACTS

The Salar lies on a plateau of the high Andes, surrounded by mountains. The salt flat itself is up to 33 ft (10 m) thick.

SALTY LAKE

Flood water on the Salar becomes eight times saltier than seawater.

SALT MINING

Every year, about 27,000 tons of salt is mined from Salar de Uyuni.

LITHIUM SOURCE

The Salar contains about 50% of the world's lithium, a metal used in batteries.

SALT BRICKS

Hotels are built on the Salar from salt bricks; they must be repaired when it rains.

CONTAINS ABOUT
11
BILLION TONS OF SALT DEPOSITS

FAIRYTALE LANDSCAPE
Sculpted by the forces of wind and water, these extraordinary rocky spires tower over the semi-arid landscape. The rock is so soft that many of the towers were hollowed out by people to form houses.

DREAMLAND
FAIRY CHIMNEYS

In the heart of Turkey lies an amazing landscape that looks like a setting for a fantasy story. The terrain is dotted with clusters of hoodoos—spires of soft rock topped by conical caps of harder rock that protect the spires from the elements. Known as fairy chimneys, they are made of compacted volcanic ash capped by solidified lava. These rocks once formed continuous layers, but rainwater seeping through cracks in the hard lava flow eroded them into isolated rocky pinnacles. Each one can survive for thousands of years, but eventually its protective cap falls off, allowing the softer rock to be worn away.

AT A GLANCE

- **LOCATION** Göreme National Park, Cappadocia, central Turkey
- **AREA** 116 sq miles (300 sq km)
- **AGE** The volcanic rocks erupted about 3 million years ago
- **STATUS** World Heritage Site

STATS AND FACTS

Over a period of at least 2,000 years, houses, churches, monasteries, and even underground cities have been carved from the volcanic rocks of Cappadocia.

CAPPADOCIA

Cappadocia comes from a Persian word meaning "land of beautiful horses."

HEIGHT

Some of the chimneys of Cappadocia are 130 ft (40 m) high.

ANCIENT LANDS

People have settled in the region since before the time of the Roman Empire.

UNDERGROUND CITY

Turkey's largest underground city, Derinkuyu, had living space for up to 20,000 people.

FORMIDABLE FORMATIONS

VALLEY OF THE MOON

Picked out by the dawn light, the rugged cone of a smoking Andean volcano looms high over the Valley of the Moon in the eastern Atacama Desert. In the foreground, white salt crystals are all that remain of an ancient lake that dried out long ago in the arid desert climate.

LETHAL LANDSCAPE

ATACAMA DESERT

Few places on Earth are as dry as the Atacama Desert in Chile. Some parts of this barren, rocky land have not seen rain for at least 50 years. This makes the desert the most hostile environment for life outside central Antarctica. The only living things in the driest parts are dormant bacteria—the same type of organisms that may exist on Mars. In fact, the desert resembles the Martian surface so closely that it has been used to test rover vehicles sent to explore the red planet.

AT A GLANCE

- **LOCATION** Northern Chile
- **AREA** At least 41,000 sq miles (105,000 sq km)
- **DESERT TYPE** Rocky and salty
- **AVERAGE RAINFALL** Less than 0.6 in (15 mm) per year

STATS AND FACTS

600 MILES (960 KM) ALONG THE COAST OF CHILE

EXTENT

The desert formed in a region cut off from moist oceanic air by mountains.

CLEAR SKIES

For more than 300 days a year, the Atacama has totally clear skies.

RAINFALL

The desert has been without significant rainfall for at least 3 million years.

TEMPERATURE

 Daytime temperatures can reach 104°F (40°C); at night they may fall to 41°F (5°C).

°C	10	20	30	40
°F	50	68	86	104

AVERAGE WIDTH

LESS THAN 100 MILES (160 KM)

DRIEST HOT DESERT

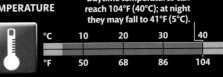

MUSHROOM ROCK

This desert rock was once half-buried and worn away just above ground level by wind-blown sand. Now exposed, its broad base is being cut away by the same sand-blaster effect.

WIND-CARVED SCULPTURE
WHITE DESERT

In the bone-dry wastes of the Farafra Depression in North Africa, the landscape is dotted with unearthly rock sculptures. They were originally created in a wet climate more than 12,000 years ago, when naturally acid rainwater dissolved the surrounding limestone. As the region turned to desert, dry sand whipped into the air by the wind attacked the rock. Since the sand grains are too heavy to be lifted high off the ground, they attack only the lower parts of the rocks. As a result, many of them have been scoured into mushroom shapes that look as if they have sprouted overnight from the dry terrain.

AT A GLANCE

- **LOCATION** Western Desert, Egypt, North Africa

- **AREA** 116 sq miles (300 sq km)

- **LANDFORM** Limestone karst

- **FORMATION** Water erosion in the past, followed by wind erosion

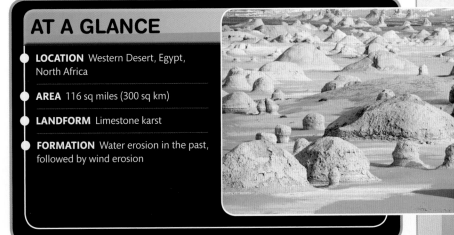

STATS AND FACTS

Rocks that have been eroded by sand carried on the wind, such as those in the White Desert, are called ventifacts. They are nearly always found in desert terrain.

DESERT BED

Fossil sea shells show that the limestone rock was formed on an ancient seabed.

WIND EROSION

The wind erosion has occurred since the region became a desert about 7,000 years ago.

TEMPERATURE

Summer temperatures can reach as high as 116°F (47°C).

°C	10	20	30	40	50
°F	50	68	86	104	122

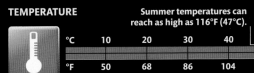

WORLD'S LARGEST STONE FOREST

ROCKY REFUGE

Tall trees grow in the gaps between the stone pinnacles, and the rocks form a refuge for rare animals—including Madagascan lemurs that leap from rock to rock, avoiding the sharp edges.

LIMESTONE BLADES
FOREST OF KNIVES

In western Madagascar, an immense sheet of limestone has been transformed into thousands of knife-like vertical blades by the erosive power of tropical rain. The naturally acidic rainwater has seeped into cracks and dissolved the rock. This has created an extraordinary stone forest of limestone pinnacles divided by deep canyons, and a hidden network of limestone caves. The pinnacles have dangerously sharp edges, and locally this terrain is known as Tsingy, or "where you cannot walk barefoot."

AT A GLANCE

- **LOCATION** Tsingy de Bemaraha National Park, Madagascar
- **AREA** 255 sq miles (660 sq km)
- **CLIMATE** Tropical
- **STATUS** Protected as a World Heritage Site due to its unique landscape and wildlife

STATS AND FACTS

200 MILLION YEARS AGO

FORMATION

The Tsingy de Bemaraha is one of two stone forests in Madagascar.

PINNACLES

UP TO **230** FEET (70 M) HIGH

CAVES

The cave network beneath the stone forest remains largely unexplored.

LEMURS

Eleven species of lemur that are endemic to Madagascar live in the stone forest.

HIKING

The rocks are so sharp that they can pierce the soles of hiking boots.

REPTILES

More than 30 species of reptile live among the stone pinnacles.

FRACTURED CONTINENT
GREAT RIFT VALLEY

Most of the spreading rifts in Earth's crust lie on the ocean floor. But one passes right through Africa, and is tearing it apart—East Africa is pulling away from the rest of the continent, opening up a vast rift valley that extends from Mozambique to the Red Sea. The valley contains some of the deepest lakes in the world.

Splitting Africa in two

The western branch of the East African Rift Valley forms the western frontiers of Uganda, Rwanda, and Tanzania. Sinking continental crust in the valley floor has created a chain of deep lakes, including Lake Tanganyika, the world's second deepest lake. Molten rock erupting through the thin, stretched crust has also formed many volcanoes.

Magma rising through the Rift Valley floor has fueled the eruption of the Virunga volcanoes.

The largest rift lake in Africa, Lake Tanganyika is up to 4,820 ft (1,470 m) deep.

The crust beneath Lake Tanganyika is sinking into the rift. Sediments on the lake bed are sinking with it.

As the crust pulls apart it fractures, creating huge faults that allow the rock to slip downwards.

The continent of Africa is pulling apart, stretching and thinning the crust above the mantle plume.

A heat current rising through Earth's deep mantle creates an extra-hot mantle plume beneath the rift.

GIANT STEPS

As the eastern side of the Great Rift Valley pulls away from the western side, huge slabs of rock sink into the rift. This has created a series of giant steps in the African landscape on each side of the valley. Each step is a block of continental crust that has slipped down a near-vertical fault, and the fault forms the steep cliff behind it.

TOWERING CLIFFS
The Torok River cascades over a cliff on the western side of the Rift Valley in Kenya. The cliff marks one of the main faults that created the valley.

> **"Every year, Africa gets a little closer to splitting into two continents."**

The Great Rift Valley is one of the few places in the world where a continent is being pulled apart. In many millions of years' time, East Africa will become an island continent in the Indian Ocean.

RIFTING

The two sides of the Rift Valley are pulling apart at the rate of about 28 in (71 cm) a century.

CRUST

The continental crust beneath the Rift Valley is five times thinner than usual for Africa.

DEPTH

In places, the valley floor lies 8,860 ft (2,700 m) below the land on each side.

PEOPLE

Fossil remains of some of our earliest ancestors have been found in the Rift Valley.

ACTIVE VOLCANOES

IN THE RIFT VALLEY

30

The Great African Rift is visible from space as a giant scar in the continent.

The crust pulls apart.

Blocks of crust sink down fault lines into the rift.

The lake fills the bottom of the rift valley.

RIFT FORMATION

The continental crust of the rift zone is being stretched, so it is thinner than usual. Hot mantle rock below the thin crust makes it swell upward, but the tension has also made it fracture, creating fault lines. These allow blocks of crust to slip downward, creating the Rift Valley and its deep lakes.

Hot mantle rises under the crust.

The opening rift in the crust eases pressure on the hot mantle rock below, allowing some to melt and form fluid magma.

AT A GLANCE

LOCATION The Y-shaped Rift Valley is in East Africa, extending from the Afar region in the north to the mouth of the Zambezi River in the south

LENGTH 2,500 miles (4,000 km)

AGE The rift started opening up 30 million years ago

FORMATION TYPE Continental rift zone

FORMIDABLE FORMATIONS

RIFT VALLEY LAKE

Lake Turkana in Africa's Eastern Rift Valley
has formed in a hollow in the sinking valley
floor. As the moving plates of Earth's crust
pull the rift apart, the tension makes cracks
open up in the rock. This allows molten rock
to boil up and erupt as volcanoes, forming
lava flows of black basalt. The lake water is
tinted green by vast numbers of microscopic
algae that flourish in the tropical heat.

LOST WORLD
MOUNT RORAIMA

Surrounded on all sides by sheer cliffs that tower above the steamy rainforests, Mount Roraima is the highest of the South American tabletop mountains known as tepuis. Its summit is a huge slab of hard, ancient sandstone, which was once part of a plateau linking Mount Roraima to other tepuis in the region. It now stands isolated—its flat summit almost inaccessible to people and wildlife alike. As a result, Mount Roraima is the home of several species of animal and plant found nowhere else. This isolation inspired Arthur Conan Doyle's 1912 novel *The Lost World*, in which explorers discover dinosaurs still surviving on top of a very similar mountain.

AT A GLANCE

- **LOCATION** On the border of Venezuela, Brazil, and Guyana
- **HEIGHT** 9,219 ft (2,810 m) above sea level
- **AREA** 12 sq miles (31 sq km)
- **CLIMATE** Tropical cloud forest

STATS AND FACTS

1884
FIRST CLIMBED

The tepuis of this region are some of the world's oldest rock formations.

FORMATION
ABOUT
2
BILLION YEARS AGO

RAINFALL
It rains almost every day on the summit of Mount Roraima.

RORAIMA TOADS
The tiny pebble toads of Roraima cannot jump very far; they roll into a ball to escape.

CLIFF HEIGHT
Mount Roraima's cliff face is more than 1,300 ft (400 m) high.

TRIPLE BORDER
About 85% of Roraima lies in Venezuela, 10% in Guyana, and 5% in Brazil.

"The word **tepui** means **house of the gods** in the local Pemón language."

MISTY MOUNTAIN

Mount Roraima is often surrounded by dense clouds, adding to its isolation. The summit rocks are deeply eroded by relentless rain, which spills off the mountain in dramatic waterfalls.

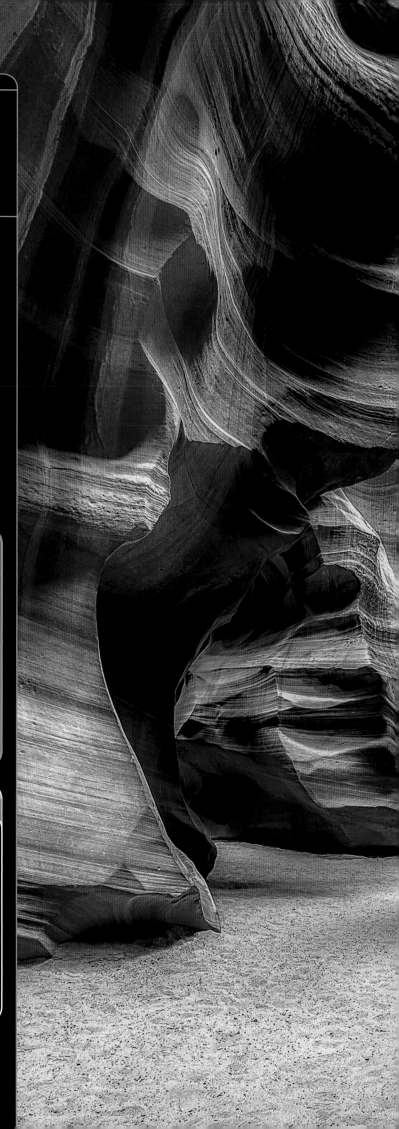

STORM DRAIN
ANTELOPE CANYON

Deserts are created by drought—long periods when there is so little rain that most plants cannot grow. But even deserts are occasionally hit by rainstorms. As there are so few plants to soak it up, the water surges over the bare ground in flash floods. Loaded with sand and rocks, these torrents gouge deep channels in the terrain as they cascade downhill. Antelope Canyon in the American Southwest is one of the most spectacular of these slot canyons—a narrow gash in the desert sandstone, carved into sinuous shapes by the raging floodwater. But for most of the year the canyon is bone dry, with no hint of the forces that created it.

AT A GLANCE

- **LOCATION** Northern Arizona
- **TYPE** Slot canyon
- **FORMATION** Eroded by flash floods
- **AGE** The sandstone of the canyon is more than 180 million years old

STATS AND FACTS

MORE THAN
1,300
FEET
(400 M)

LENGTH

Antelope Canyon is carved into rock that was once a desert sand dune.

DEPTH

ABOUT
120
FEET
(37 M)

WATER SURGE

A desert storm can flood the canyon in just a few minutes.

RAINFALL

The land around the canyon receives as little as 2 in (5 cm) of rain per year.

TEMPERATURE

Temperatures in the canyon can rise up to 100°F (38°C) in summer.

°C		10	20	30	40
°F	50		75		100

WATER SCULPTURE
Sunlight filtering down into the narrow canyon makes the layered sandstone glow with rich color. Swirling currents of sand-loaded water have scoured the bare rock for thousands of years.

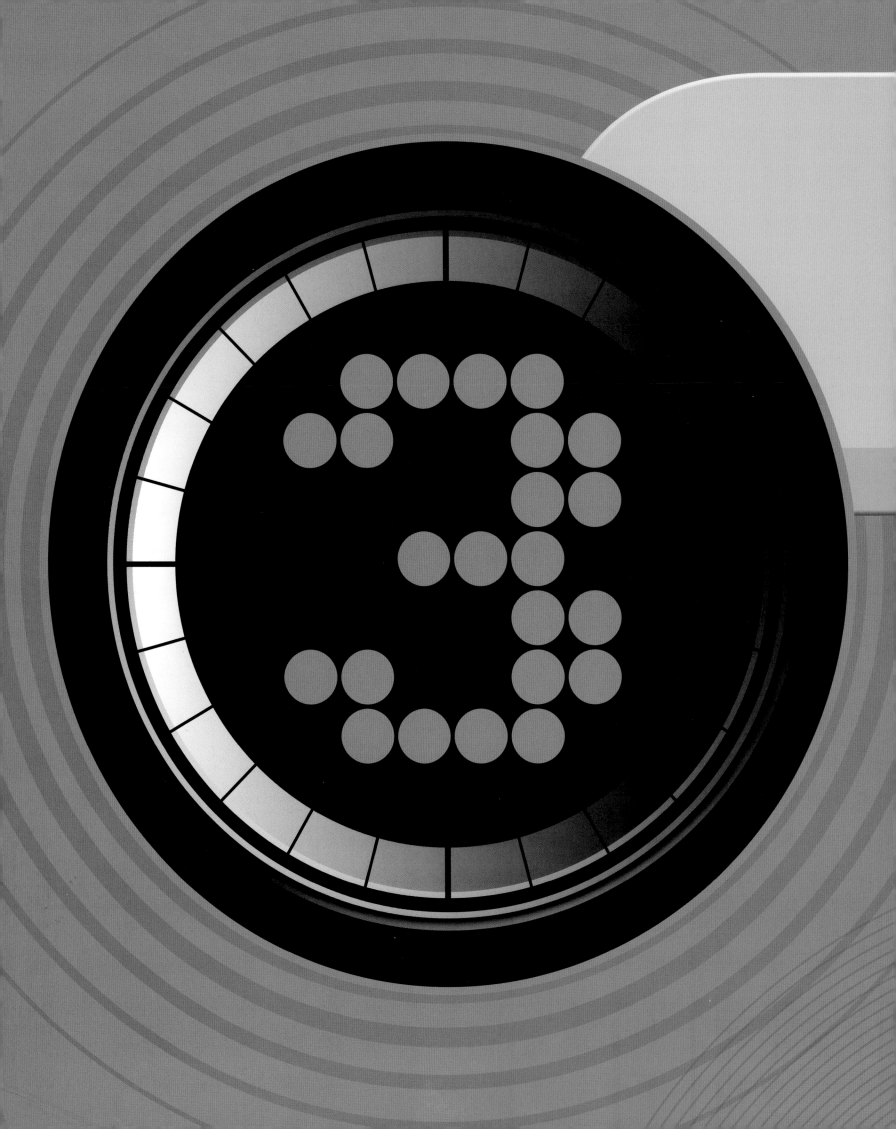

FIRE AND STEAM

Whether they are erupting molten rock in spectacular fountains of fire, or exploding with catastrophic power, volcanoes are the most dramatic evidence of Earth's restless nature. The forces that create volcanoes also fuel the hot springs and geysers that boil up from volcanic zones.

RIVERS OF FIRE
KILAUEA

The big island of Hawaii is a mass of huge volcanoes. These have erupted from the Pacific Ocean floor, which lies 18,000 ft (5,500 m) below the waves. Kilauea is the youngest and most active volcano—a simmering pot of basalt lava that regularly boils over and flows away from the volcano in rivers of liquid fire, all the way to the coast. The lava often solidifies at the surface but continues to flow underneath the solid rock, pouring downhill in streams of molten basalt that spill into the sea amid clouds of steam. The liquid lava flows so fast and so far that it has formed a broad, gently sloping shield volcano rather than a steep cone.

AT A GLANCE

- **LOCATION** Hawaii
- **VOLCANO TYPE** Oceanic shield volcano
- **AREA** 579 sq miles (1,500 sq km)
- **HEIGHT** 4,091 ft (1,247 m) above sea level

STATS AND FACTS

Five volcanoes have combined to form the big island of Hawaii—Hualalai, Kilauea, Kohala, Mauna Kea, and Mauna Loa. These form the highest volcanic complex on Earth.

SURFACE

About 70% of the volcano's surface is formed of lava flows less than 600 years old.

VOLCANIC ACTIVITY

The eruption that started in January 1983 continues today, flowing down to the sea.

AGE OF VOLCANO

Kilauea is 600,000 years old, but appeared above sea level about 100,000 years ago.

TOTAL HEIGHT

Kilauea's total height from the Pacific Ocean floor is over 22,150 ft (6,750 m).

OLDEST EXPOSED LAVA

2,800 YEARS OLD

FIRE FOUNTAIN

A fiery fountain of molten basalt rock explodes from Kilauea's most active vent. This vent is part of a long rift in the volcano's eastern side that has been erupting continuously since 1983.

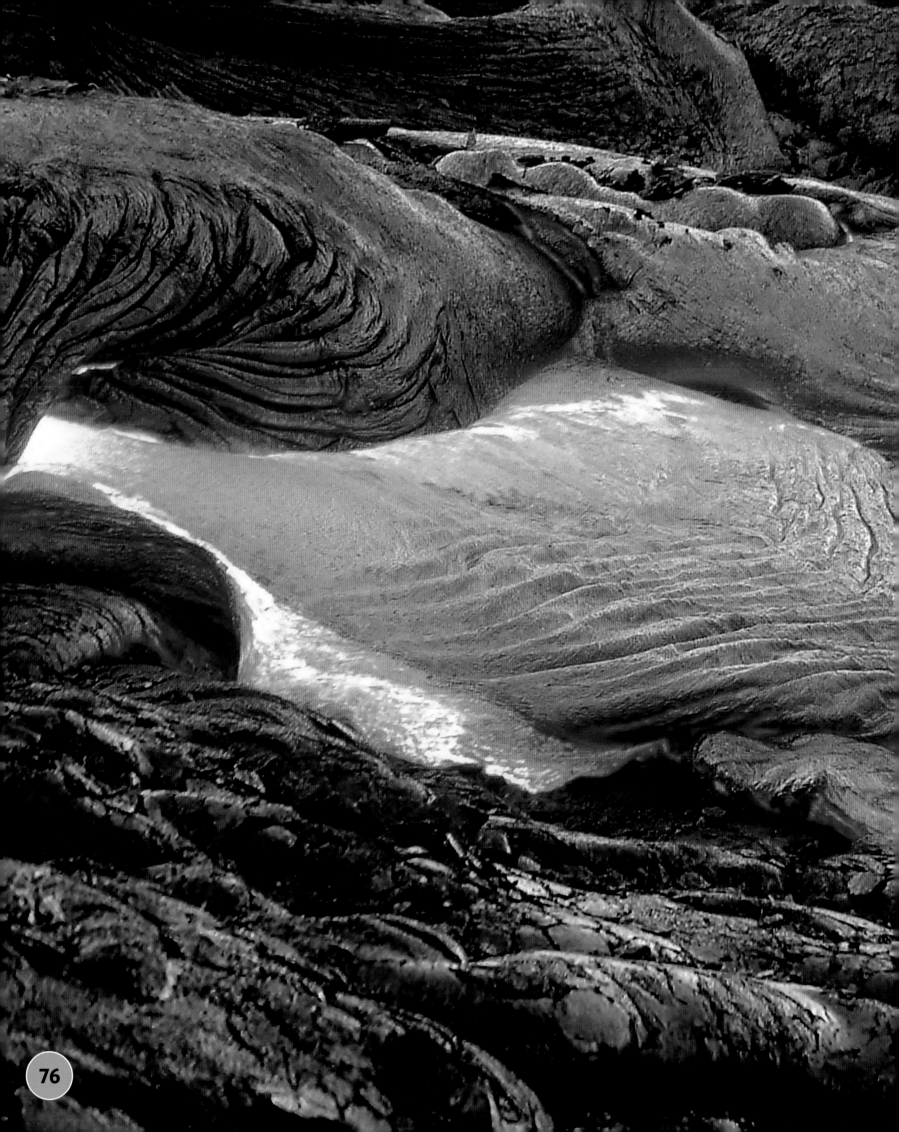

LAVA FLOW

Made of melted ocean-floor bedrock, the basalt lava erupting from Kilauea is more liquid than the sticky lava that erupts from typical volcanoes. It flows rapidly across the island before cooling and turning to solid rock. The surface of the lava cools first, often forming a wrinkled skin of black basalt as the hot, liquid lava beneath it keeps flowing.

VOLCANIC HOTSPOT
HAWAIIAN ISLAND CHAIN

The active volcanoes of Hawaii are part of a chain of islands and submerged seamounts that extends across the Pacific Ocean to Russia. Each of its volcanoes has erupted over the same hotspot beneath the moving ocean floor. The plate movement carries the islands northwest, away from the hotspot, so the volcanoes stop erupting and gradually sink below the waves.

Trail of volcanoes

The Hawaiian islands have been created by a plume of heat rising through Earth's deep mantle. This heat makes the ocean-floor rock melt and form gigantic volcanoes. As the ocean floor creeps slowly northwest, each volcano falls extinct, and a new one starts erupting over the stationary hotspot.

This island has sunk below sea level, forming a flat-topped seamount called a guyot.

Kauai is the oldest of the main islands. Its volcano last erupted 500,000 years ago.

The deeply eroded volcanoes on Oahu have been extinct for 10,000 years.

Heat currents in the upper mantle are dragging the Pacific Plate very slowly across the globe.

Earth's mantle is made of heavy, very hot rock. It is solid, but flows very slowly, like putty.

AT A GLANCE

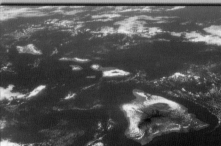

- **LOCATION** Central Pacific Ocean
- **VOLCANO TYPE** Oceanic shield volcano
- **LENGTH** The Hawaiian island chain is 1,490 miles (2,400 km) long
- **HEIGHT** The summit of the highest volcano, Mauna Kea, is 13,802 ft (4,207 m) above sea level.

STATS AND FACTS

The Hawaiian island chain has 132 volcanic islands and atolls. The chain extends northwest in the form of over 80 extinct underwater volcanoes—known as the Emperor Seamount chain.

MOVING PLATE

The Pacific Plate moves northwest by about 4 in (10 cm) a year.

HIGHEST MOUNTAIN

If measured from the base on the ocean floor to its summit, Mauna Kea is the highest mountain on Earth.

ISLAND CHAINS

Combined, the Hawaiian island and the Emperor Seamount chain stretches over 3,600 miles (5,800 km).

SEAMOUNTS

The youngest seamount, Loihi, began forming about 400,000 years ago; the oldest named seamount, Meiji, is 85 million years old.

SINKING ISLANDS

As a volcanic island is carried off the hotspot and stops erupting, the rock beneath it cools down. The rock shrinks as it cools, and this makes the island start sinking. Coral reefs that have formed around it sink too, but so slowly that the coral can grow upward at the same rate. Eventually, the original volcano disappears, leaving just a ring of coral called an atoll.

1

Volcanic island

A hotspot volcano forms a cone of volcanic rock. This stands on the ocean floor, which is pushed up by the hot mantle rock below.

2

Island sinks

Earth's crust sinks as it cools below an extinct volcano, but surrounding coral keeps growing. Meanwhile, the cone is eroded by the weather.

3

Atoll forms

All the volcanic rock above sea level vanishes, but the coral reef forms a ring of sandy islands around a central lagoon—an atoll.

Hawaii's Big Island lies above the hotspot, which fuels eruptions from its two southern volcanoes.

Kilauea volcano on the southern flank of the island is the world's most active volcano.

The huge volcanoes that form Hawaii rise from the ocean floor.

A new volcano called Loihi is erupting from the ocean floor just south of Hawaii. Eventually, it will form a new island.

Maui has moved off the hotspot—its volcano last erupted about 200 years ago.

At the top of the hot mantle plume the rock melts, and erupts from volcanoes.

COLOSSAL ISLAND ASSEMBLY LINE

LAKE OF FIRE
ERTA ALE

One of the world's most active volcanoes, Erta Ale is located at the northern end of the African Rift Valley, where Earth's crust is being torn apart by the Arabian Plate ripping away from Africa. Molten rock welling up from beneath the crust forms a fiery lake of liquid basalt lava, which churns and bubbles like boiling water. At the lake surface the lava cools to form a brittle rocky shell. But this is constantly fracturing and sinking to give glimpses of the glowing molten lava below. Every few years a surge of activity makes the lava lake boil up and spill over on to the surrounding landscape, where the lava has built up a broad shield volcano of dark basalt rock.

AT A GLANCE

- **LOCATION** Afar Triangle, Ethiopia, northeast Africa
- **VOLCANO TYPE** Shield volcano
- **VOLCANO WIDTH** 31 miles (50 km)
- **HEIGHT** 2,011 ft (613 m)

MOLTEN GLOW

The true nature of Erta Ale's lava lake becomes clear as night falls. The crater is lit up by the glow of the searingly hot lava beneath the thin crust of dark rock at the surface.

LONGEST LASTING LAVA LAKE

STATS AND FACTS

480
FEET
(150 M)
LAVA LAKE DIAMETER

Erta Ale is just one of six lava lakes in the world and it's the most active.

LAST MAJOR ERUPTION
2007

LAVA LAKE

The lava lake has been a feature of the volcano for about 110 years.

ERTA ALE

In the local Afar language, Erta Ale means "Smoking Mountain."

LAVA TEMPERATURE

1,830°F (1,000°C)

°C	500	1,000
°F	1,000	2,000

PAINTED POOLS
DALLOL HOT SPRINGS

Dallol in Ethiopia is an alien landscape of vividly colored hot springs that are fueled by the heat of a hidden volcano. The whole area is a vast salt flat almost a mile deep, dotted with steaming fumaroles and simmering pools fed by hot springs. Salt, sulfur, potash, and iron erupting from the fumaroles and hot springs have created fields of colored minerals. Some of these minerals dissolve in water to form pools of greenish sulfuric acid. Lying well below the sea level in the blistering heat of the Danakil Depression, Dallol is one of the most hostile places on Earth.

AT A GLANCE

- **LOCATION** Danakil Depression, Ethiopia, northeast Africa
- **FORMATION** Hydrothermal field in salt flat
- **ELEVATION** 148 ft (45 m) below sea level
- **AVERAGE TEMPERATURE** 93°F (34°C)

STATS AND FACTS

The hot springs of Dallol are at the north end of the Great Rift Valley in the Danakil Depression, the lowest point in Africa. Part of the Depression lies 328 ft (100 m) below sea level.

MINERALS

The salt fields supply nearly 100 percent of Ethiopia's salt.

FUMAROLES

The air smells of rotten eggs due to the hydrogen sulfide released by the fumaroles.

TEMPERATURE

Maximum temperature in June reaches 116°F (47°C).

°C	20	40	60
°F 50	100		150

DALLOL VOLCANO

LAST ERUPTED IN
1926

COLORFUL CRYSTALS
Chemical-rich water evaporating in the searing heat of Dallol leaves behind thick deposits of salt crystals. These crystals are stained with rusty red iron, yellow sulfur, and other minerals. Dark cinder cones dotting the skyline mark the sites of small volcanic eruptions.

HOTTEST INHABITED PLACE ON EARTH

BOILING MUD
ROTORUA

New Zealand is an earthquake zone, where one plate of Earth's crust is grinding against another. The Pacific Ocean floor is pushing beneath North Island, and this is ripping the island apart, opening a great rift down its center. Magma welling up beneath the rift has caused colossal volcanic eruptions in the past, creating huge, crater-like calderas that now contain lakes such as Lake Taupo and Lake Rotorua. Within the calderas, heat from below makes boiling water emerge in hot springs, geysers, and bubbling mudpots. Some of the most spectacular erupt around the city of Rotorua, sometimes called Sulfur City because of all the volcanic gases in the air.

AT A GLANCE

- **LOCATION** Taupo Volcanic Zone, North Island, New Zealand

- **AGE** Rotorua caldera was formed about 230,000 years ago

- **MAIN FEATURES** Mudpots, hot springs, and geysers

- **GEOTHERMAL ACTIVITY** Constant

STATS AND FACTS

The Taupo Volcanic Zone is a dormant supervolcano, like Yellowstone in the US. It has the same history of massive eruptions that have had a global impact.

ROTORUA TOWN

The entire town of Rotorua (population 57,800) lies within the Rotorua caldera.

TAUPO ZONE

The last supervolcanic eruption in the zone occurred 26,500 years ago.

RIFT LENGTH

The rift that created the calderas is 217 miles (350 km) long, extending into the Pacific Ocean.

km	250	300	350	400
miles	150	200		250

AREA OF CALDERA

31
SQ MILES
(80 SQ KM)

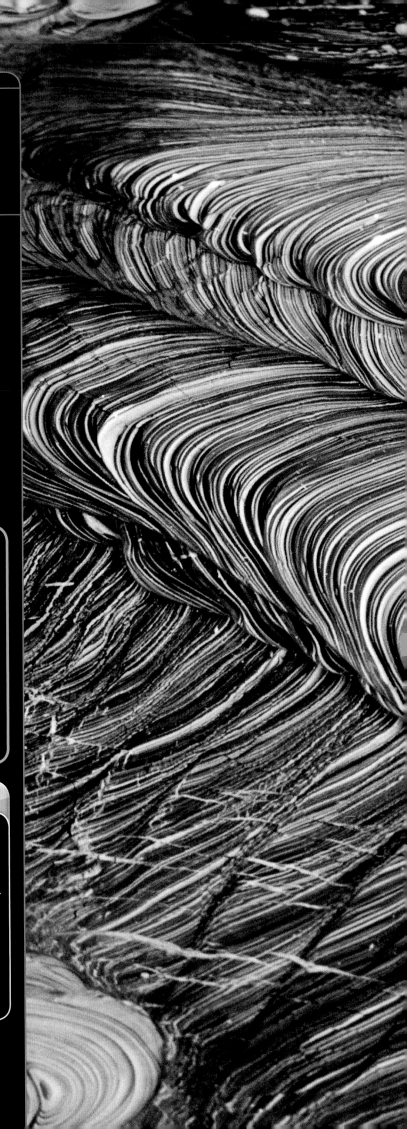

MUD BUBBLES

Dazzling patterns of circular ripples are created by volcanic gas bubbling up through mud at Rotorua. The sulfurous gas mixes with water to form sulfuric acid, which attacks rocks and turns them to mud.

BLISTERING HEAT

BLACK SMOKERS

On parts of the ocean floor, jets of searingly hot water erupt into the near-freezing darkness. They boil up from the rifts in Earth's crust that form mid-ocean ridges. Rising magma beneath each rift heats the ocean-floor rocks, in turn heating the seawater that has seeped into it. Intense pressure allows the water to dissolve minerals, which turn into dark, smoky particles when the hot water erupts into the cold ocean.

- **LOCATION** On mid-ocean ridges, such as the East Pacific Rise and Mid-Atlantic Ridge
- **DEPTH** Average 6,890 ft (2,100 m) below waves
- **SIZE** A black smoker chimney may be more than 130 ft (40 m) high
- **FORMATION** Chimneys built of minerals dissolved from ocean-floor rocks

Minerals dissolved in the hot water turn to sooty particles when they hit cold seawater.

STATS AND FACTS

The minerals erupted by black smokers and similar ocean-floor vents are vital to all oceanic life.

VENTS FIRST FOUND

1977 ON THE EAST PACIFIC RISE

TEMPERATURE
Water spurting from the smokers can be as hot as 867°F (464°C).

GROWTH RATE
A black smoker can grow at a rapid rate of 12 in (30 cm) a day.

SUPER DEEP
The deepest known black smokers lie about 16,500 ft (5,000 m) below the ocean surface.

VENT FIELDS
The largest vent field, known as TAG, is the size of a soccer stadium.

HOTTEST WATER ON EARTH

Billowing vent

Water that filters down to the ocean-floor rock is heated before being forced back up into the ocean. When the erupting water mixes with the cold seawater, the minerals solidify. Some of these billow up like smoke; others build up chimneylike structures around the vents. Remarkably, the minerals also support vast colonies of specialized animals such as crabs, mussels, and giant tubeworms.

Vent water that has been superheated under pressure erupts from the chimney into ocean water that is close to freezing point.

Layers of different minerals are deposited as the hot water cools in the chimney.

LIFE IN THE DARK

Most animals rely on food made by plants and algae using solar energy, but black smokers erupt in the deep ocean, where there is no sunlight. The extraordinary animals living around these vents rely on food made by bacteria. While the crabs eat the bacteria, other animals such as the Pacific giant tubeworms have colonies of bacteria inside their bodies and live on the food they make.

Giant tubeworms gather vital minerals using their bright red gills—they have no mouth, eyes, or even a stomach.

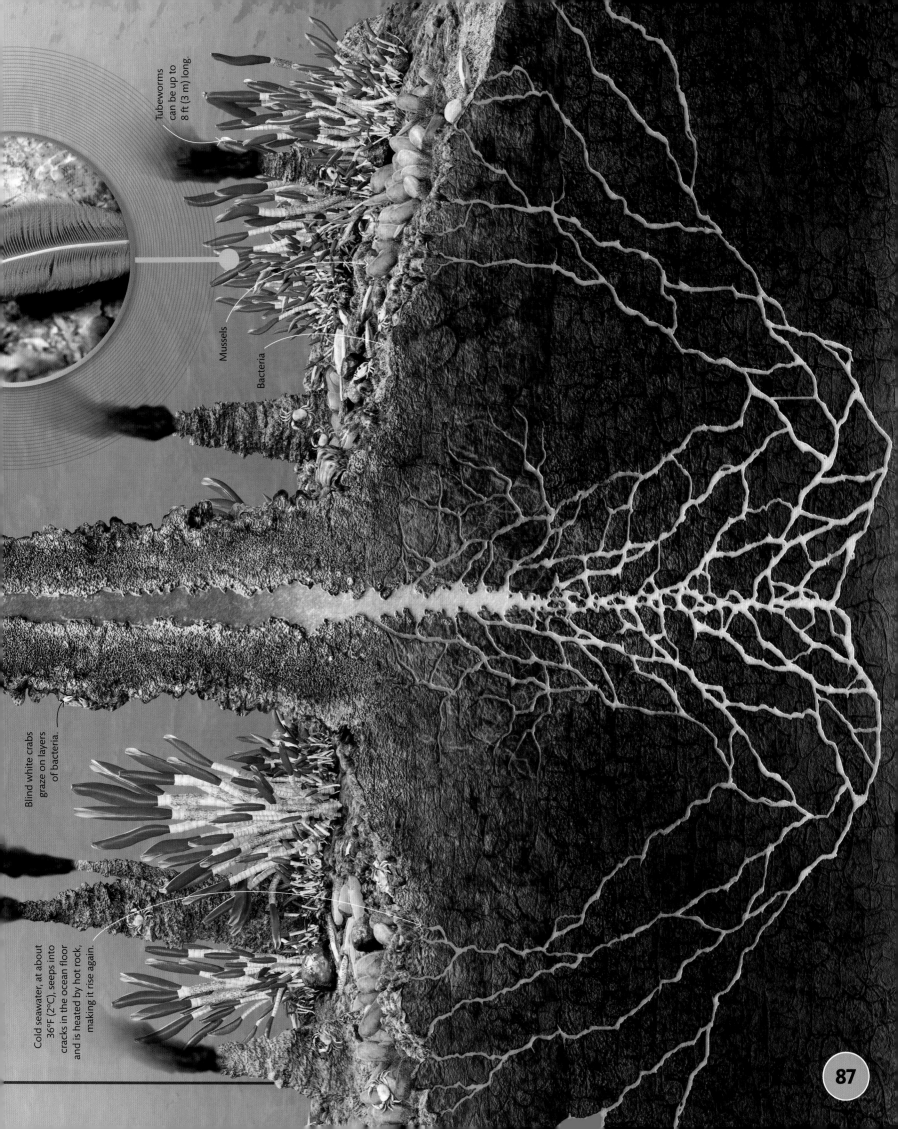

Tubeworms can be up to 8 ft (3 m) long.

Mussels

Bacteria

Blind white crabs graze on layers of bacteria.

Cold seawater, at about 36°F (2°C), seeps into cracks in the ocean floor and is heated by hot rock, making it rise again.

FIERY ISLAND
VOLCANIC JAVA

The island of Java is a mass of volcanoes that have erupted where one plate of Earth's crust is sinking beneath another. Water carried down with the sinking crust changes the chemistry of the hot rock below, making it melt and triggering the eruption of volcanoes along the plate boundary. Where this happens on the ocean floor, chains of volcanic islands called island arcs are formed, sometimes joining up to form bigger islands like Java. These volcanoes produce sticky gas-filled lava that may flow from the crater or explode into the air in huge ash clouds. The ash and lava build up in layers to form steep-sided cones known as stratovolcanoes.

"Indonesia has 130 active volcanoes."

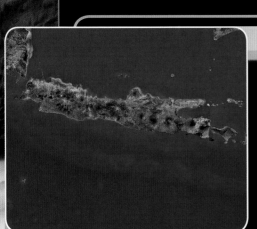

AT A GLANCE

- **LOCATION** Java, Indonesia
- **VOLCANO TYPE** Stratovolcanoes
- **MAXIMUM HEIGHT** Mount Semeru rises to 12,060 ft (3,676 m)
- **AGE** Java formed from erupting volcanoes within the last 2–3 million years

STATS AND FACTS

Java is part of the Sunda Arc – one of the most volcanic regions on Earth. The most catastrophic eruptions in recent history—Tambora (1815) and Krakatoa (1883)—have occurred on the Sunda Arc close to Java.

JAVA

Java has 45 active volcanoes, and many more are dormant, but not extinct.

MOUNT SEMERU

Semeru, the highest volcano on Java, has ash explosions every 10–30 minutes.

MOUNT MERAPI

Merapi has produced more pyroclastic flows than any other volcano on Earth.

SUPER CLUSTER

Most volcanoes on Java are only about 50 miles (80 km) apart.

CLUSTERED CONES

A chain of volcanoes forms the backbone of Java. Five of these volcanoes have erupted in the caldera (collapsed crater) of a much bigger volcano that exploded 45,000 years ago. They form the Bromo volcanic landscape—the most spectacular evidence of Java's fiery nature.

VOLATILE VOLCANO
MOUNT ETNA

Looming over the Mediterranean island of Sicily, Mount Etna is one of the world's most active stratovolcanoes. Its regular eruptions have built up a vast cone of ash and lava, high enough to be capped with snow in winter. But the frequent eruptions also act as safety valves, releasing pressure that might otherwise cause much bigger, more dangerous eruptions. So, despite its volatile nature, Etna is not as violent as it looks.

Ash cloud
Unusually, Etna erupts in many different ways. Some eruptions unleash rivers of liquid molten rock, while others are more explosive, producing billowing clouds of volcanic ash, and raining lava bombs on to the slopes below.

Magma forced between rock layers has formed shallow magma chambers.

Searing hot ash and gas cascade downhill in pyroclastic flows.

Eruptions from small vents and fissures have created hundreds of cinder cones, such as this one.

AT A GLANCE

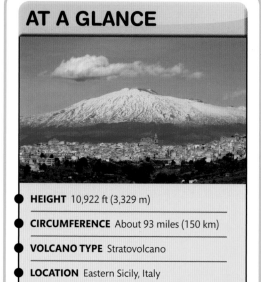

- **HEIGHT** 10,922 ft (3,329 m)
- **CIRCUMFERENCE** About 93 miles (150 km)
- **VOLCANO TYPE** Stratovolcano
- **LOCATION** Eastern Sicily, Italy

STATS AND FACTS

ABOUT 500,000 YEARS AGO
FORMATION

One of the world's most complex volcanoes, Mount Etna is also the biggest and most active in Europe.

NEARBY POPULATION

More than 25% of Sicily's population live on Etna's slopes.

0% 10% 20% 30% 40% 50%

VOLCANIC ACTIVITY

The volcano has erupted about 200 times in the last 3,500 years.

SMOKE RINGS

Etna's summit craters emit giant smokelike rings that are made of steam.

MOST VIOLENT ERUPTION
MARCH 1669

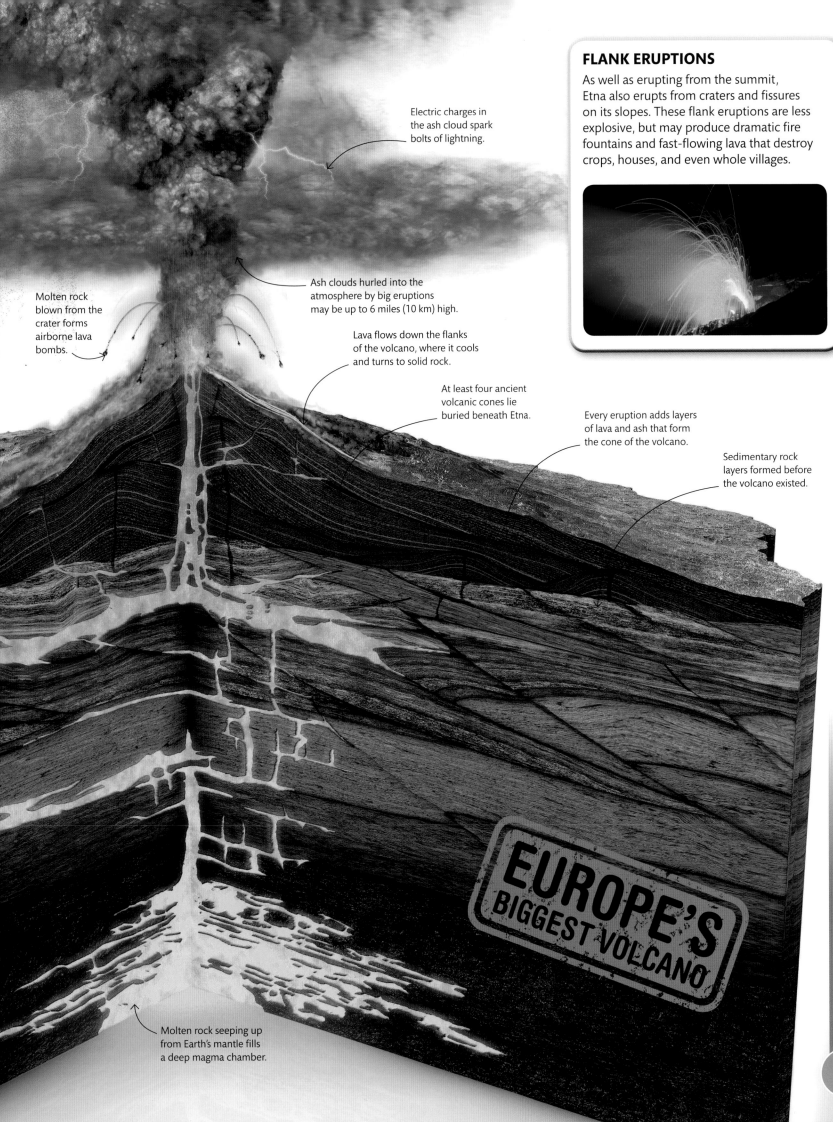

Electric charges in
the ash cloud spark
bolts of lightning.

FLANK ERUPTIONS

As well as erupting from the summit,
Etna also erupts from craters and fissures
on its slopes. These flank eruptions are less
explosive, but may produce dramatic fire
fountains and fast-flowing lava that destroy
crops, houses, and even whole villages.

Molten rock
blown from the
crater forms
airborne lava
bombs.

Ash clouds hurled into the
atmosphere by big eruptions
may be up to 6 miles (10 km) high.

Lava flows down the flanks
of the volcano, where it cools
and turns to solid rock.

At least four ancient
volcanic cones lie
buried beneath Etna.

Every eruption adds layers
of lava and ash that form
the cone of the volcano.

Sedimentary rock
layers formed before
the volcano existed.

EUROPE'S
BIGGEST VOLCANO

Molten rock seeping up
from Earth's mantle fills
a deep magma chamber.

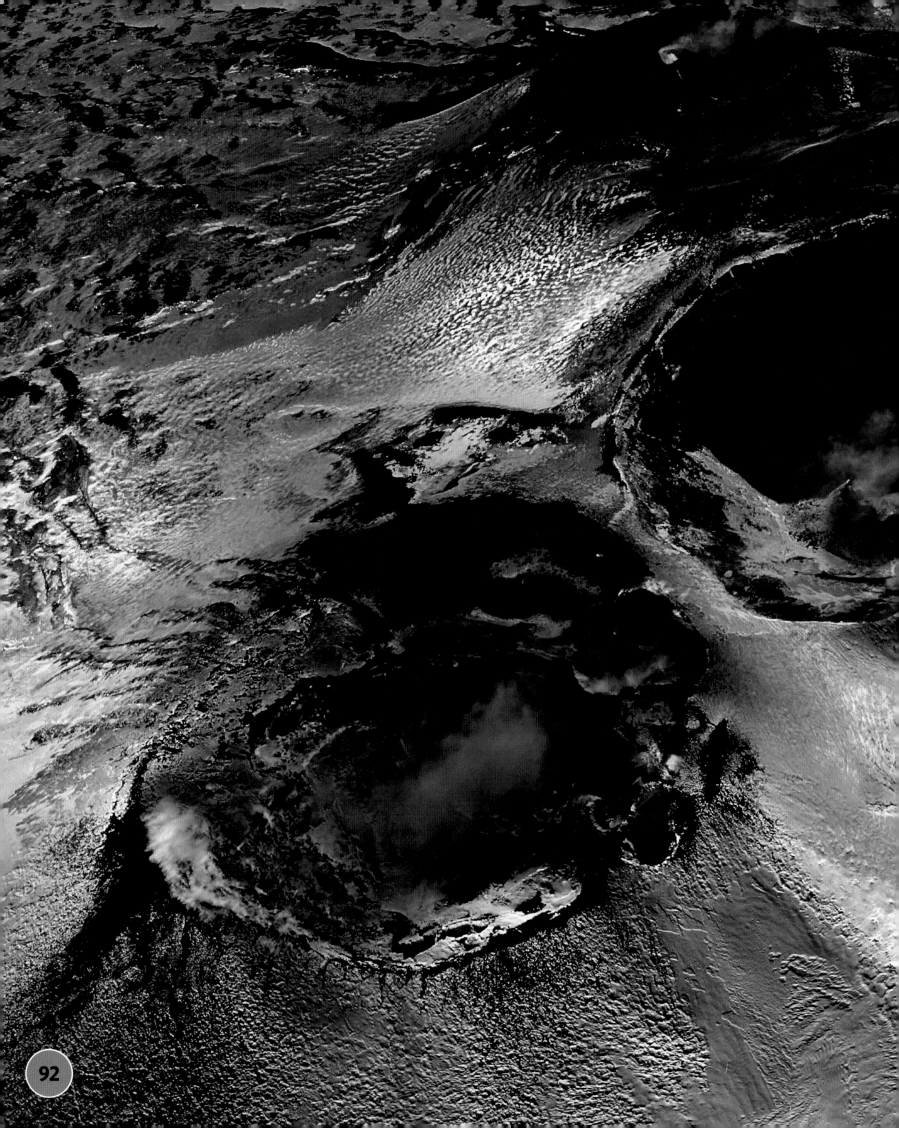

SMOKING SUMMIT

Two thousand years ago a massive eruption destroyed the summit of Mount Etna, creating a broad depression that has slowly filled with lava. There are four active craters within this summit caldera, which erupt explosively to blast columns of volcanic ash and gas high into the air. In winter, the surrounding slopes are white with snow.

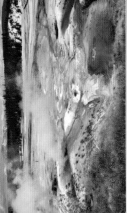

SUPERVOLCANO
YELLOWSTONE CALDERA

Deep beneath the spectacular wilderness of Yellowstone National Park lies a simmering supervolcano—a gigantic mass of molten rock that could erupt with enough force to cause global chaos. It has done so in the distant past, filling the atmosphere with volcanic dust. As the magma chamber emptied, the ground above collapsed into it, forming a broad depression known as the Yellowstone caldera. Today, this has many hot springs and geysers, fuelled by the heat below.

This entire area of Yellowstone National Park is 3,472 square miles (8,991 sq km).

Parts of the caldera floor are being forced up into shallow domes by the swelling magma below.

Yellowstone Lake lies in the lowest part of the caldera at the heart of Yellowstone National Park.

Sleeping giant
Yellowstone lies above a hotspot in Earth's mantle—a huge, mobile mass of extra-hot rock that rises from near the planet's core. This mantle plume is solid, but flows very slowly. At the top, reduced pressure allows some of the hot rock to melt and flow into a magma chamber deep in Earth's crust below Yellowstone. This feeds a shallower magma chamber that lies beneath the Yellowstone caldera.

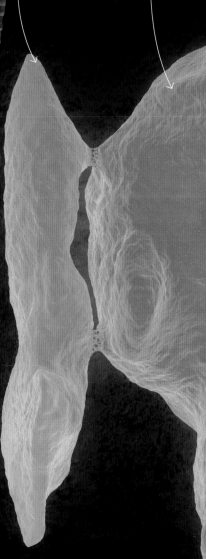

A shallow magma chamber beneath the caldera heats groundwater. This water erupts as hot springs and geysers.

The lower magma chamber contains a mixture of hot, semi-molten, spongy rock, and liquid magma.

Molten rock forming at the top of the mantle plume rises through cracks in the brittle crust to fill a huge magma chamber.

The very hot rock of the mantle plume is kept solid by intense pressure, but is soft enough to flow slowly.

GLOBAL THREAT

Yellowstone last erupted 640,000 years ago, with a catastrophic explosion that blasted 230 cubic miles (1,000 cubic km) of rock into the air. It could happen again, creating enough volcanic ash to cover half of the USA. Airborne haze would shroud the globe, dimming the Sun and chilling the climate.

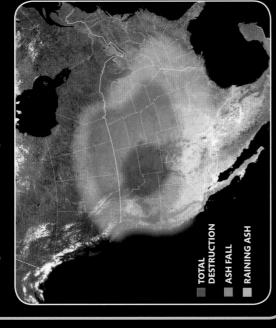

- ■ TOTAL DESTRUCTION
- ■ ASH FALL
- ■ RAINING ASH

STATS AND FACTS

Scientists watch Yellowstone very carefully, and luckily, it shows no signs of erupting soon.

ACTIVITY

Two-thirds of the world's hot springs and geysers erupt in Yellowstone's caldera.

TEMPERATURE

Yellowstone's magma chamber has a temperature of about 1,400°F (760°C).

MANTLE PLUME

Scientists think that Yellowstone's mantle plume may rise from near Earth's outer core.

CALDERA SIZE

A huge city such as Tokyo, one of the biggest in the world, could fit inside the caldera.

BIGGEST KNOWN ERUPTION

2.1 MILLION YEARS AGO

HEAT AND LIFE

Tiny figures on the walkway show the scale of Yellowstone's Grand Prismatic Spring—one of the largest hot springs on Earth. In the blue center, water bubbles up from below ground at up to 188°F (87°C). As the water spreads it cools, allowing the growth of microbes that vary in color depending on the temperature of the water.

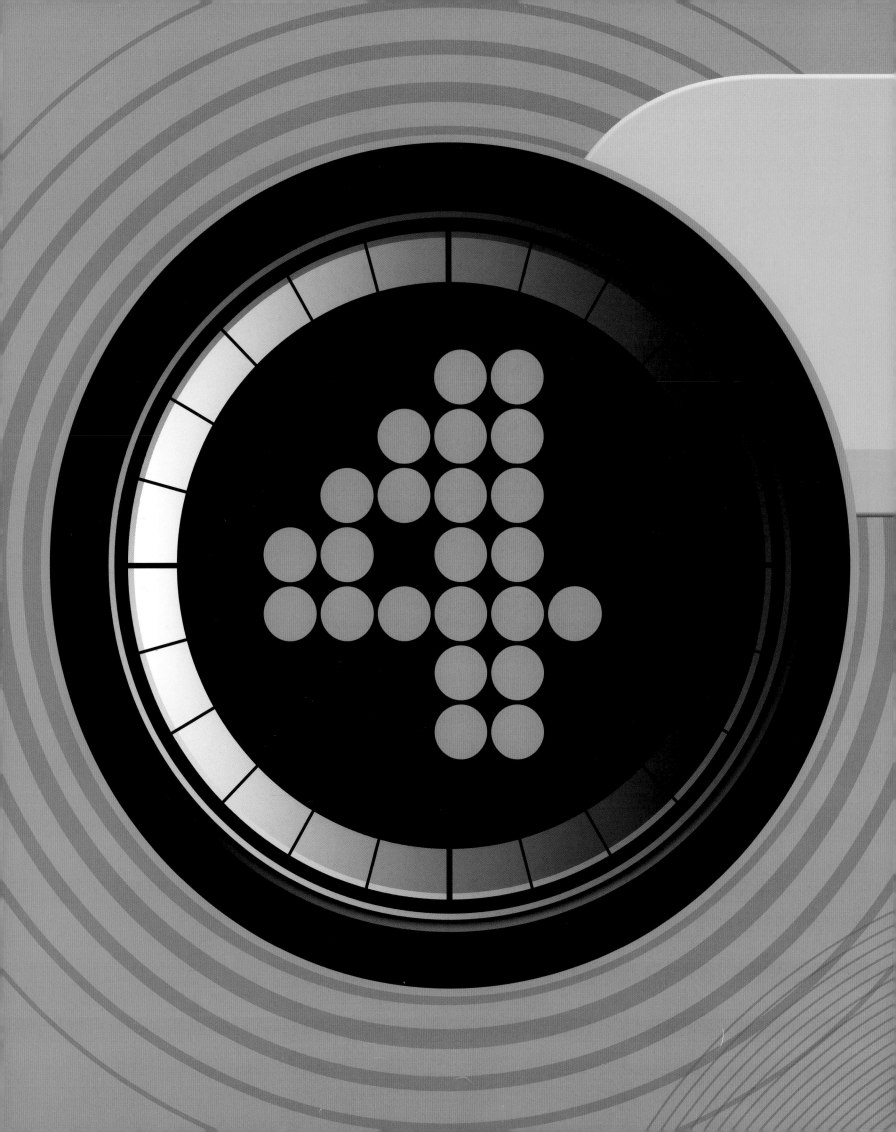

FROZEN WORLD

Almost 70 percent
of Earth's fresh water is frozen
into solid ice. Most of it forms ice
sheets and glaciers in the Arctic,
Antarctic, and high mountains.
But just a few thousand years ago,
these ice sheets were far larger.
The land they once covered
still bears the scars of
these ice ages.

RIVER OF ICE
KASKAWULSH GLACIER

On mountains and in the polar regions, temperatures stay so low throughout the year that snow never melts. Instead, it builds up in deep layers that are compressed into ice by their own weight. The heavy ice creeps slowly downhill as a glacier, such as the Kaskawulsh Glacier in western Canada. It grinds through rock to create deep valleys, carrying away heaps of shattered rock on the surface. Small glaciers may join together to form broader ones and, in cold climates, these may flow all the way to the sea. The Kaskawulsh Glacier terminates in the St Elias Mountains, where its meltwater flows away as rivers.

AT A GLANCE

- **LOCATION** Kluane National Park, Yukon Territory, Canada

- **LENGTH** 47 miles (75 km)

- **MAXIMUM WIDTH** 3.7 miles (6 km)

- **STATUS** Retreating to the point where one of the rivers fed by its meltwater is drying up

STATS AND FACTS

Like many glaciers all over the world, the Kaskawulsh Glacier is getting shorter because its ice is melting at a higher altitude due to climate change.

ICE THICKNESS

 The ice of the Kaskawulsh Glacier is up to 3,280 ft (1,000 m) thick.

AREA

 The glacier covers more than 9,650 sq miles (25,000 sq km) of mountain terrain.

RATE OF FLOW

 The glacier ice flows at a speed of about 500 ft (150 m) per year.

m	50	100	150
ft	160	330	500

ICE AND ROCK

Two glaciers merge to form the mighty Kaskawulsh Glacier. Dark ribbons of rubble ripped from the valley sides are carried on the ice; if they reach the end of the glacier they help build up a big mound called a terminal moraine.

VANISHED GLACIER

A gigantic glacier once filled this valley in Montana. Loaded with rock fragments, a colossal weight of moving ice gouged a deep trough through the mountains, and then completely melted away.

CARVED BY ICE

ICE-AGE SCARS

For at least 2 million years, Earth has been in the grip of ice ages. We are now living in a relatively warm period, with ice only in the polar regions and in high mountain ranges. But 22,000 years ago, much of northern North America and northern Eurasia were shrouded by ice sheets and glaciers. As the ice melted, it left dramatic scars in the landscape, especially in the rocky uplands. These include deep U-shaped valleys and glacial lakes carved by glaciers, vast scree slopes of frost-shattered rock, and heaps of rocky debris known as moraines. In fact, nearly all the mountain landscapes that are most admired today were shaped by ice.

AT A GLANCE

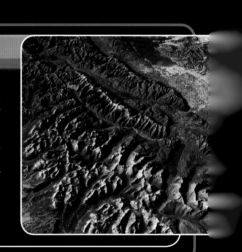

- **LOCATION** North America, Eurasia, Patagonia, and New Zealand

- **FORMATION** Erosion by ice that has since melted

- **AGE** More than 10,000 years old

- **LARGEST GLACIAL FEATURES** The Great Lakes

STATS AND FACTS

During the coldest part of the most recent ice age, so much water turned to continental ice that global sea levels fell by up to 400 ft (120 m). Thick ice sheets in the Northern Hemisphere spread as far south as Seattle and New York in the US, and Berlin in Germany.

GLACIAL ICE

Today, 10% of Earth's land is covered with ice, compared to 32% in the last ice age.

FRESH WATER

About 70% of Earth's fresh water is stored as glacial ice.

SEA LEVEL

If all the glacial ice melted, the global sea level would rise by 230 ft (70 m).

CANADA

About 20,000 years ago, 97% of Canada was entirely covered by ice.

SHEER DROP
NORWEGIAN FJORDS

During the last ice age, many glaciers flowing to the coast across the icebound mountains of Scandinavia gouged such deep valleys in the landscape that they were below sea level. When the glaciers finally melted, the water they released raised the global sea level by up to 330 ft (100 m), flooding the U-shaped troughs scooped out by the ice to create fjords. Like all glaciated valleys, they have very steep rocky walls that are often almost vertical, and which plunge straight into the cold northern water to great depths. Many Norwegian fjords are deeper than the nearby sea; huge ocean-going ships can sail up them, dwarfed by the towering cliffs.

AT A GLANCE

- **LOCATION** Western Norway
- **WATER DEPTH** Typically more than 1,000 ft (330 m)
- **LENGTH** The longest Norwegian fjord extends for 127 miles (205 km)
- **AGE** Most were created more than 10,000 years ago

STATS AND FACTS

In total, there are about 1,190 fjords in Norway and nearby Svalbard. They form the world's most dramatic coastal landscapes.

REEFS

Norwegian fjords have some of the largest cold-water coral reefs.

ROAD TUNNELS

Huge tunnels have been constructed under the fjords to facilitate transport.

COASTLINE

Norway's coastline is 18,000 miles (29,000 km) with the fjords, but only 1,550 miles (2,500 km) without them.

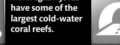

km (in 1,000)	5	10	15	20	25

miles (in 1,000)	5	10	15

DEEPEST FJORD

4,291 FEET (1,308 M)

THE POWER OF ICE

Carved out of granite by a gigantic glacier more than 12,000 years ago, Lysefjord in southern Norway is overlooked by sheer cliffs towering at least 1,970 ft (600 m) above the water.

ICE CAVES
MENDENHALL GLACIER

Glacier ice that forms high in the mountains creeps slowly downhill until it reaches an altitude where the air and surrounding rock are warm enough to melt it. This makes a steady stream of meltwater flow from beneath the end of the glacier. In Alaska, this melting process has created long tunnels and caves in the base of the Mendenhall Glacier. At this depth, the glacier ice is very dense, having been compressed by the colossal weight of ice pressing down on it from above. The dense ice absorbs long-wavelength red light from the sunlight that filters down into the cave, making its icy walls and ceilings glow with a clear, luminous blue.

AT A GLANCE

- **LOCATION** Southeastern Alaska
- **GLACIER LENGTH** 13.7 miles (22 km)
- **GLACIER STATUS** Retreating because of climate change
- **ICE CAVES** Fast melting away

STATS AND FACTS

The caves beneath Mendenhall Glacier have formed in ice created from snow that fell on Alaska's Juneau Icefield many centuries ago.

GLACIER SOURCE

Mendenhall Glacier is one of the 38 large glaciers that flow from the Juneau Icefield.

FROZEN TREES

Melting ice has revealed tree stumps frozen for more than 1,000 years.

AREA

At 1,500 sq miles (3,885 sq km), the Juneau Icefield is the fifth largest icefield in North America.

sq km	1,000	2,000	3,000
sq miles	500	1,000	1,500

AGE OF CAVE WALLS

UP TO
250
YEARS
OLD

INTO THE BLUE

As the ancient ice melts beneath the snout of the Mendenhall Glacier, flowing meltwater carves a network of spectacular ice caves. These are always changing in shape, and may soon vanish altogether.

FROZEN CONTINENT
ANTARCTICA

The continent of Antarctica is the coldest place on Earth. It was once the home of dinosaurs that roamed through green forests, but the relentless forces of plate tectonics carried the land mass to the South Pole where it was transformed into an icy wasteland. Most of Antarctica's rocky continent is buried deep beneath vast ice sheets that spill out over its freezing coastal seas.

Rock and ice

If the thick ice could be lifted off Antarctica it would reveal a continent divided in two by the rugged Transantarctic Mountains. Much of the continental rock lies below sea level, weighed down by the colossal weight of ice. The thickest ice occurs near the South Pole on East Antarctica.

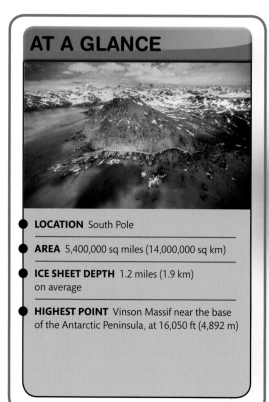

AT A GLANCE

- **LOCATION** South Pole
- **AREA** 5,400,000 sq miles (14,000,000 sq km)
- **ICE SHEET DEPTH** 1.2 miles (1.9 km) on average
- **HIGHEST POINT** Vinson Massif near the base of the Antarctic Peninsula, at 16,050 ft (4,892 m)

The Antarctic Peninsula extends toward the tip of South America. Its icy mountains are fringed by rocky tundra.

The floating Ronne Ice Shelf is part of the West Antarctic Ice Sheet that spills out over the Weddell Sea.

Like the Ronne Ice Shelf, the Ross Ice Shelf is a vast sheet of floating ice. Huge pieces regularly break away to form gigantic icebergs.

Weddell Sea

SOUTHERN OCEAN

Ross Sea

Antarctica is surrounded by the stormy Southern Ocean, which freezes over in winter.

West Antarctica has a ridge of mountains covered by a sheet of ice, which extends out to sea as floating ice shelves.

Pulverized rock carried off the continent by moving ice covers the bed of the Ross Sea.

STATS AND FACTS

With temperatures that would freeze your skin within seconds, Antarctica is the coldest place on Earth and as a result, the least explored. It is also the highest, driest, and windiest of the continents.

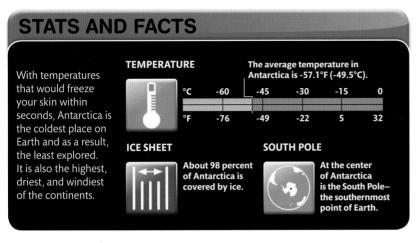

TEMPERATURE

The average temperature in Antarctica is -57.1°F (-49.5°C).

°C	-60	-45	-30	-15	0
°F	-76	-49	-22	5	32

ICE SHEET

About 98 percent of Antarctica is covered by ice.

SOUTH POLE

At the center of Antarctica is the South Pole—the southernmost point of Earth.

The Transantarctic Mountains stretch right across Antarctica. They form one of the longest mountain ranges on Earth.

Near the heart of the frozen continent, the East Antarctic Ice Sheet is 3 miles (4.8 km) thick.

Owing to the thickness of the ice sheets, the average altitude of Antarctica is more than 13,120 ft (4,000 m) above sea level.

The lowest areas of the continental bedrock have been pushed below sea level due to the weight of the ice.

East Antarctica is higher and colder than the western side of the continent.

ICY OCEAN

Every winter the sea around Antarctica freezes over. It forms a vast tract of floating sea ice that covers an area bigger than the continent itself. Most of it is drifting pack ice driven by the ocean currents, but forming an almost continuous sheet.

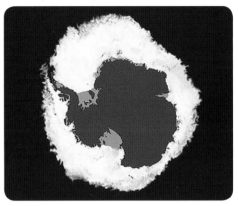

WINTER ICE EXTENT

The winter sea ice around Antarctica covers up to 7 million sq miles (18 million sq km) of ocean. It reaches its maximum extent in September, at the end of Southern Hemisphere winter.

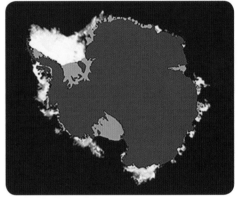

SUMMER ICE EXTENT

In spring, the sea ice starts melting, and by late February, it covers just 1.2 million sq miles (3 million sq km). Most of this summer ice is swept clockwise around the Weddell Sea by wind-driven currents.

WORLD'S LARGEST ICE SHEET

TOWERING ICE SHELF

Where the vast ice sheets that shroud Antarctica spill out over the ocean, they form gigantic floating ice shelves. The biggest, the Ross Ice Shelf, is the size of France. The immensely thick floating ice forms a sheer cliff that is more than 370 miles (600 km) long, and towers up to 164 ft (50 m) above the surface of Antarctica's Ross Sea.

"As **icebergs** melt, compressed air bubbles within the ice **pop** with a fizzing sound."

TIP OF THE ICEBERG
Just the tip of this Antarctic iceberg floats above the waves of the cold Southern Ocean, where its dense blue ice provides a safe refuge for a group of Adélie penguins.

DRIFTING ICY ISLANDS
ICEBERGS

In the polar regions, the cold climate enables glaciers to flow all the way to the coast, spilling out into the sea as floating tongues of ice. As the tides rise and fall, they fracture the glaciers so pieces snap off, tumble into the sea, and drift away as icebergs. Many are quite small, but some icebergs are colossal floating islands that can drift for years in the ocean currents before melting away. They are a serious hazard to shipping, as the fate of the giant ocean liner *Titanic* proved in 1912.

AT A GLANCE

- **LOCATION** Cold oceans
- **FORMATION** Fragments of glaciers that have drifted out to sea
- **SIZE** The largest known iceberg was bigger than Belgium
- **LONGEVITY** Up to five years

STATS AND FACTS

Most icebergs occur in the North Atlantic near Greenland, and in the Southern Ocean around Antarctica.

HIDDEN ICE

Ninety percent of an iceberg's bulk is hidden; just 10 percent is visible.

BREAKING AWAY

Every year, up to 50,000 big icebergs break away from the glaciers of Greenland.

TEMPERATURE

An iceberg may have a core temperature lower than -4°F (-20°C).

°C	-20	0	20
°F	0	25	50

HEIGHT

UP TO
525
FEET
(160 M)
ABOVE SEA
LEVEL

GLITTERING FROST GARDEN
FROST FLOWERS

In places with very cold winters, seas and lakes freeze at the surface where the water is chilled by the cold air. While the ice is still thin, it releases water vapor that forms a layer of moist air just above the ice. If this is then chilled by contact with very cold air, the moisture can freeze back onto the ice in crystals that grow into glittering frost flowers. They can grow only if the air is much colder than the ice below so, as the ice gets thicker and colder, the frost flowers stop forming.

AT A GLANCE

- **LOCATION** Anywhere with standing water that freezes over in winter

- **FORMATION** Caused by water vapor freezing into ice crystals

- **PURITY** Lake frost flowers are pure water; on sea ice they are full of salt

- **SURVIVAL** They normally last for only a few days

STATS AND FACTS

Frost flowers grow on thin ice, and cannot form on thicker, colder ice. They can be found on new sea ice in the polar regions.

TEMPERATURE

Air temperature must be at least 27°F (15°C) lower than the ice for frost flowers to form.

WIND FACTOR

Another key factor is that wind speed must be below about 11 mph (18 km/h).

SIZE

The delicate frost flowers grow as high as 2 in (5 cm).

MICROBES

Each frost flower houses about a million bacteria.

FLOWERING LAKE
Very calm, cold air above
the newly frozen surface of
Lake Louise in western Canada
has triggered the growth of an
entire meadow of dazzling,
delicate frost flowers.

CRACKED ICE

Long cracks slice across the frozen surface of Lake Baikal like jet vapor trails in a clear sky. The ice is 6.6 ft (2 m) thick, and is constantly cracking with a sound like gunfire.

DEEP FREEZE
LAKE BAIKAL

Just north of Mongolia, the continent of Asia is being torn apart to create a huge rift in Earth's crust. At least 5.6 miles (9 km) deep, the rift has filled with sediment and water to form the world's deepest lake. During the bone-chilling Siberian winter, the exceptionally pure lake water freezes at the surface almost overnight, forming a vast sheet of thick ice that is as clear as glass. It freezes so fast that waves in the lake surface are frozen solid. But stresses in the ice make it crack and fracture, pushing up tumbled blocks that glow turquoise in the cold winter light.

AT A GLANCE

- **LOCATION** Southern Siberia, eastern Russia
- **LENGTH** 395 miles (636 km)
- **AREA** 12,245 sq miles (31,722 sq km)
- **MAXIMUM DEPTH** Lake bed is 5,387 ft (1,642 m) below the surface

STATS AND FACTS

Lake Baikal formed about 25 million years ago, when Earth's crust pulled apart to create a rift valley, which filled with water.

CAPACITY

Lake Baikal holds more water than the five North American Great Lakes combined.

FRESH WATER

The lake contains about 20 percent of the world's fresh water.

ACTIVE RIFT

The rift continues to widen at a rate of about 1 in (2.5 cm) per year.

cm		2		4		6		8
in			1		2			3

LAKEBED SEDIMENT

UP TO **4** MILES (7 KM) THICK

TEMPERATURE

The temperature in the area averages -6°F (-21°C) in winter and 52°F (11°C) in summer.

°C	-20	-10	0	10	20
°F	-4	14	32	50	68

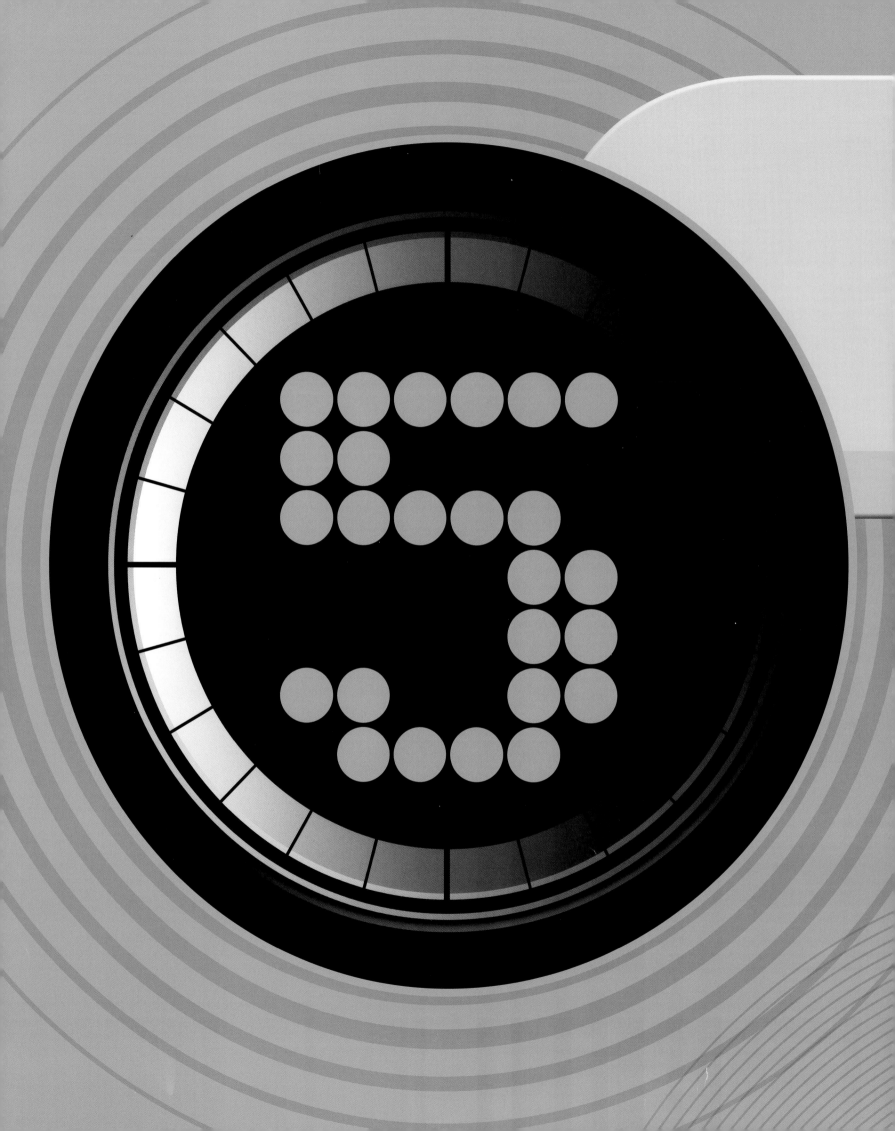

WATER WORLD

Much of Earth's landscape
has been shaped by the water
that flows off hills and mountains
in great rivers and cascading
waterfalls. Running water
levels mountains and carves deep
valleys, and the sand and silt
swept away by the flow forms
new land wherever it settles.

GIGANTIC WATERFALL
VICTORIA FALLS

In the heart of southern Africa, the mighty Zambezi River pours into a deep gorge, forming the biggest waterfall on Earth—Victoria Falls. The gorge is the first of six that carry the river away to the south along a zigzag route. The gorges have been carved into a vast sheet of hard basalt rock, which forms the lip of the waterfall. During the tropical rainy season, the entire width of the falls is a mass of roaring, tumbling water, almost obscured by billowing clouds of spray.

AT A GLANCE

- **LOCATION** On the border between Zambia and Zimbabwe
- **HEIGHT** 355 ft (108 m)
- **WIDTH** 5,604 ft (1,708 m)
- **AVERAGE FLOW** 38,423 cubic feet (1,088 cubic m) per second

STATS AND FACTS

10,594 CUBIC FEET (300 CUBIC M)

MIN FLOW PER SECOND

The Victoria Falls were named by Scottish explorer David Livingstone in 1855.

MAX FLOW PER SECOND

452,000 CUBIC FEET (12,800 CUBIC M)

RAINY SEASON VOLUME

Enough water cascades to fill an Olympic-sized swimming pool every two seconds.

SPRAY

The tall cloud of spray can be seen from 30 miles (48 km) away.

AREA

The Victoria Falls cover an area equal to 25 soccer fields.

ROYAL NAME

The falls were named after the British monarch, Queen Victoria.

WORLD'S LARGEST WATERFALL

THUNDERING SPRAY

Sunlight glinting through the rising spray forms a rainbow over the Victoria Falls, known locally as *Mosi-oa-Tunya*, or "the smoke that thunders." The spray often rises 1,300 ft (400 m) above the waterfall.

COLOSSAL CAVE
HANG SON DOONG

WORLD'S BIGGEST CAVE

The gigantic Hang Son Doong in Vietnam is the world's largest known cave, with a main passage big enough to contain a 40-story skyscraper. Hidden by thick jungle, the cave was not discovered until 1991. Like all limestone caves, it was created by naturally acidic rainwater seeping down through cracks in the rock and slowly dissolving it. Where the water drips off the cave roof, the dissolved minerals turn back into limestone, forming spectacular stalagmites, stalactites, and a 200-ft (60-m) high wall that all but blocks one end of the cave. Two huge sinkholes, each measuring about 330 ft (100 m) across, allow life-giving light into the darkness of the cave.

AT A GLANCE

- **LOCATION** Quang Binh Province, central Vietnam

- **LENGTH** Main cave system is more than 5.6 miles (9 km) long

- **WIDTH** Up to 490 ft (150 m)

- **MAXIMUM HEIGHT** More than 660 ft (200 m)

STATS AND FACTS

Limestone caves occur all over the world. As more are explored every year, an even bigger cave than Hang Son Doong may yet be found.

CHAMBER SIZE

The main chamber is large enough to contain a 747 Jumbo Jet.

TREE LIFE

The cave's two giant chambers have 100-ft (30-m) high trees growing inside.

STALAGMITES

Up to 230 ft (70 m) high, the cave has the world's tallest known stalagmites.

CAVE NETWORK

Altogether, there may be more than 150 chambers in the cave.

AGE OF CAVE

UP TO
5
MILLION
YEARS OLD

SUPER-SIZED

The tiny figure of a cave explorer is dwarfed by the monumental size of the cavern. A tropical forest grows in a giant sunlit cavity created where part of the cave roof has collapsed.

AT A GLANCE

- **LENGTH** More than 4,000 miles (6,400 km)

- **WIDTH** Main channel up to 25 miles (40 km) wide

- **AVERAGE FLOW** 7,381,000 cubic ft (209,000 cubic m) per second

- **SOURCE** Peruvian Andes

MAJESTIC RIVER

Dense tropical rainforest surrounds the rivers of the Amazon basin. Each rainy season at least 93,000 sq miles (240,000 sq km) of the forest is flooded as the river level rises by more than 30 ft (9 m).

TROPICAL FOREST GIANT

AMAZON RIVER

The mighty Amazon River flows across South America from the Andes to the Atlantic. Fed by at least 1,100 tributary rivers draining off a region the size of Australia, the Amazon carries far more water to the ocean than any other river. Its course takes it through the world's biggest tropical rainforest—a wildlife paradise with more species of plants and animals than any other habitat. The river itself is also teeming with life, from river dolphins to fearsomely voracious red-bellied piranhas.

STATS AND FACTS

Fed by the largest drainage basin in the world, covering 40 percent of South America, the Amazon River accounts for a fifth of global river flow into the oceans.

RECORD BREAKER

As well as being the largest river, the Amazon is also the widest river in the world.

DEPTH

In some places the river is as much as 330 ft (100 m) deep.

VOLUME

In the rainy season, the flow reaches 11 million cubic ft (300,000 cubic m) per second.

cu m	200,000	300,000	400,000
cu ft (in millions)	7	11	

AGE OF RIVER

ABOUT **11** MILLION YEARS OLD

GLITTERING SALT LAKE
DEAD SEA

DEEPEST SALT LAKE

Occupying a deep depression near the eastern shore of the Mediterranean, the salt lake known as the Dead Sea is the world's lowest point on land. River water flowing into the lake evaporates in the hot, dry climate before it can flow out again, and as the water vapor rises into the air it leaves salty minerals behind. Over thousands of years these have built up to create some of the saltiest water on Earth. The lake is called the Dead Sea because nothing can live in it, apart from a few specialized salt-loving microbes.

AT A GLANCE

- **LOCATION** Jordan Valley, bordered by Jordan, Israel, and Palestine
- **LENGTH** 31 miles (50 km)
- **WIDTH** 9 miles (15 km)
- **DEPTH** 997 ft (304 m)

STATS AND FACTS

The Dead Sea has formed in a deep valley created by a gigantic fault that divides two plates of Earth's crust.

SHRINKING LAKE

 Due to reduced flow in the river feeding it, the lake's water level is falling every year.

SALT CONTENT

 The Dead Sea is almost ten times as salty as seawater.

TEMPERATURE

 On average, the air temperature stays above 86°F (30°C) for six months a year.

DENSE WATER

 The Dead Sea's very high salt content enables swimmers to float effortlessly.

LAKE SURFACE

1,407 FEET (429 M) BELOW SEA LEVEL

CRYSTAL SHORES

The water of the Dead Sea is so salty that salt crystals form on its shores, and even in the shallows. The salt is not like that in seawater because the combination of minerals is different.

RIVER OF FIVE COLORS
CAÑO CRISTALES

The Caño Cristales in Central Colombia has been called the most beautiful river in the world. It is famous for its crystal clear waters, but more especially for the aquatic plants that grow in them. For most of the year, they are barely noticeable. But for a few months, when the water is at just the right depth, a rare water plant called *Macarenia clavigera* turns a brilliant red. Its vivid color is set off by green waterweeds, blue and black water, and yellow sand, creating a dazzling spectacle.

AT A GLANCE

- **LOCATION** Serranía de la Macarena, Colombia, South America

- **NEAREST CITY** Bogota

- **RIVER LENGTH** 62 miles (100 km)

- **TIME OF YEAR** Phenomenon occurs from August to November

STATS AND FACTS

The multicolored Caño Cristales is also known as the "River of Five Colors" or the "Liquid Rainbow." It is a fast-flowing river with many rapids and waterfalls.

RARE PLANT

The red *Macarenia clavigera* weed is found nowhere else on Earth.

RIVER LIFE

The Caño Cristales River has no fish, because the very pure water contains so little food.

PLANT SIZE

Individual *Macarenia clavigera* plants are about 2 in (5 cm) long.

	cm	2	4	6	8
	in	1	2	3	

WORLD'S MOST BEAUTIFUL RIVER

ROCKY RIVER

Red *Macarenia* weed drapes the potholes made by stones trapped in rocky cavities in the river bed. As they are rolled around by the current, the stones grind away the rock, creating the pits.

MAGICAL POOLS

Mineral-rich water from the springs spills downhill over the travertine terraces, cooling and depositing more travertine. Many of the terraces contain shallow pools of warm water.

BLUE CASCADE
PAMUKKALE

In the mountains of western Turkey, heat from molten rock deep beneath the surface has triggered the eruption of hot springs at Pamukkale, near the city of Denizli. The hot water is rich in calcium carbonate, dissolved from limestone rocks below the ground. When the water bubbles up into the air, a chemical reaction makes the calcium carbonate turn into the mineral travertine. Over thousands of years this process has built up a series of extraordinary travertine terraces that cascade down the slope like an icy staircase dripping with water. However, instead of being icy cold, the water is steaming hot, and has been used for bathing since Roman times.

AT A GLANCE

- **LOCATION** Denizli Province in southwestern Turkey
- **HEIGHT OF TERRACES** 525 ft (160 m)
- **SIZE** 1.7 miles (2.7 km) long
- **STATUS** World Heritage Site

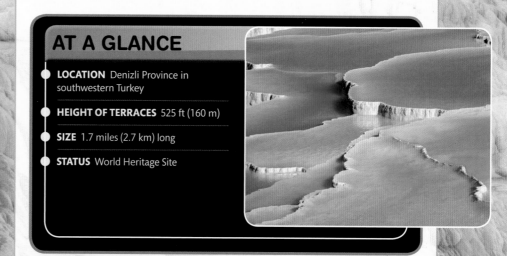

STATS AND FACTS

17
NUMBER OF HOT SPRINGS

Pamukkale is the site of Hierapolis, a health resort built by the Romans.

SPRING WATER TRAVELS

1,050
FEET
(320 M)
TO THE
TERRACES

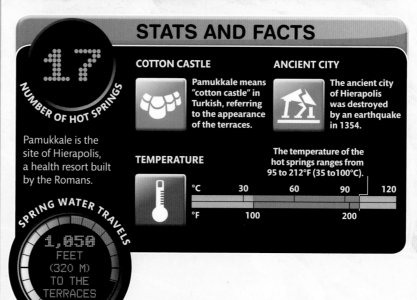

COTTON CASTLE

Pamukkale means "cotton castle" in Turkish, referring to the appearance of the terraces.

ANCIENT CITY

The ancient city of Hierapolis was destroyed by an earthquake in 1354.

TEMPERATURE

The temperature of the hot springs ranges from 95 to 212°F (35 to100°C).

°C	30	60	90	120
°F	100		200	

LIVING ROCK
GREAT BARRIER REEF

One of the most impressive rock formations on Earth, the Great Barrier Reef in Australia has been built by living organisms. For thousands of years, tropical corals have been absorbing minerals from ocean water and using them to make their stony skeletons. In the process, they have built up a huge bank of coral rock that extends the length of Australia's northeast coast.

The open tropical ocean supports far less life than the coral reef, which is one of the richest habitats on Earth.

The box jellyfish that drift around the reef have stinging tentacles for paralyzing their prey.

Glittering waters

Reef corals are animals that have microscopic plantlike algae living in their tissues. These algae use the energy from sunlight to make food, which the corals need to survive, so coral reefs can grow only in clear, sunlit water. The Great Barrier Reef has formed in the shallow water covering Australia's continental shelf, where it supports a dazzling diversity of sea life.

Powerful predators, like this tiger shark, patrol the fringes of the reef.

AT A GLANCE

- **LOCATION** Coral Sea coast of Queensland, northeastern Australia

- **TYPE** Tropical coral reef

- **AREA** 14,300 sq miles (37,000 sq km)

- **AGE** Reef started growing more than 25 million years ago

STATS AND FACTS

The Great Barrier Reef is a vast complex of almost 3,000 reefs – about the size of Italy. The reef is home to probably more wildlife species than any other habitat on Earth.

WATER TEMPERATURE

 Reef corals grow only in water with a temperature of 20–29°C (68–84°F).

EXTENT

 The Great Barrier Reef extends for a distance of at least 1,430 miles (2,300 km).

ISLANDS

 Between the edges of the mainland and the coral reef, there are more than 2,000 islands.

REEF LIFE

 The reef supports more than 600 species of coral, and 1,600 species of fish.

WORLD'S LARGEST LIVING STRUCTURE

Sheltered from big ocean waves, the reef flat teems with vividly colored fish.

A fierce hunter, the peacock mantis shrimp lives in the crevices of the reef.

Massive stony corals form the reef crest facing the open ocean.

CORAL ROCK

The continental bedrock lies deep below the reef's living surface. The rest of the reef is made of coral rock—a type of limestone formed from the star-shaped stony skeletons of billions of long-dead corals. The living reef grows on top of this mass of dead coral.

The deep reef wall is made up of dead coral that thrived thousands of years ago, when the sea level was lower.

INTO THE BLUE

At the outer edge of the reef, the coral forms a steep wall, and the shallow reef flat gives way to deep blue ocean. Off the northern Great Barrier Reef, the ocean depth drops down to at least 6,560 ft (2,000 m).

DAZZLING REEF

The Great Barrier Reef is made up of many smaller coral reefs, linked together in a complex network of reef crests surrounding shallow sandy lagoons. The gleaming white coral sand of the lagoons glows turquoise through the crystal clear tropical water. Beyond the far edge of the reef lies the deep blue of the open Pacific Ocean.

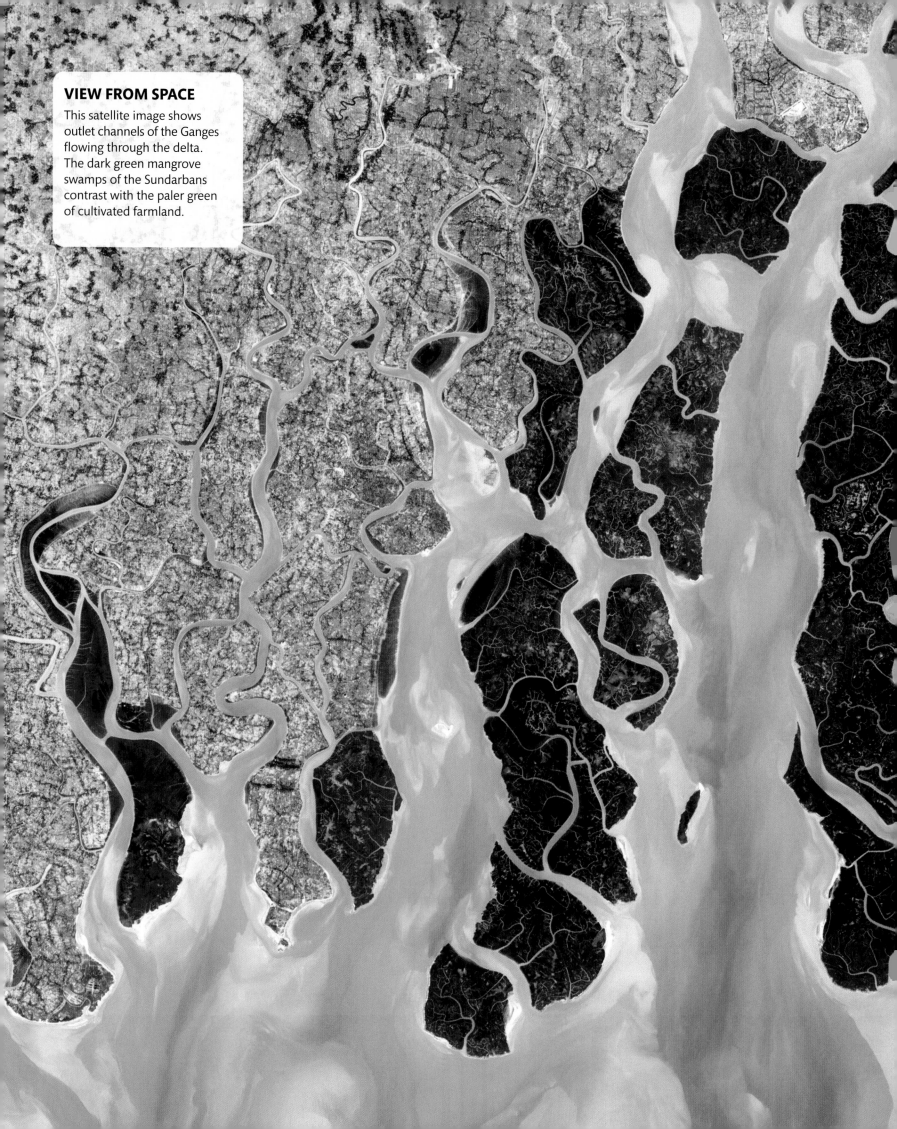

This satellite image shows outlet channels of the Ganges flowing through the delta. The dark green mangrove swamps of the Sundarbans contrast with the paler green of cultivated farmland.

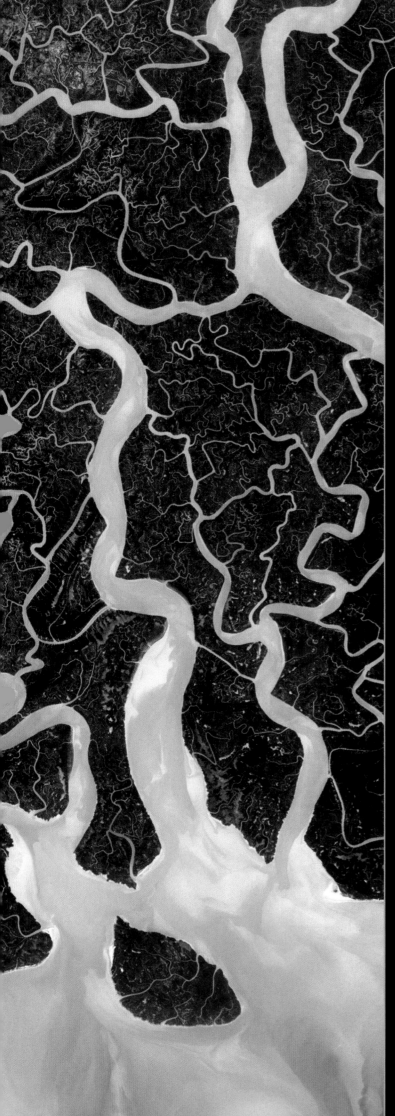

GIGANTIC SWAMP
GANGES DELTA

The Ganges and its sister river, the Brahmaputra, flow down to the Indian Ocean from the Himalayas, carrying vast amounts of silt swept off the mountains. Where these rivers flow into the sea at the Bay of Bengal, the salt water makes the silt particles clump together and settle on the seabed in thick layers. This extends the land into a low-lying fan called a delta. As the rivers flow over this they divide into complex networks of channels flanked by dense forests and mangrove swamps. The wilder parts are known as the Sundarbans, and are a haven for wildlife, including tigers. But the soil is so fertile that large areas have been turned into farmland.

AT A GLANCE

- **LOCATION** India and Bangladesh, at the northern end of the Bay of Bengal

- **MAXIMUM WIDTH** 220 miles (354 km)

- **AREA** More than 41,000 sq miles (105,000 sq km)

- **SEDIMENT DEPTH** 10 miles (16 km)

STATS AND FACTS

The delta extends under the Bay of Bengal to create a giant submarine fan. The colossal weight of sediment in the delta and fan has distorted Earth's crust.

SEDIMENT

The Ganges carries 2.2 billion tons of sediment to the sea each year.

POPULATION DENSITY

The delta is one of the world's most densely populated regions, with 143 million inhabitants.

BENGAL TIGERS

About 1,000 Bengal tigers survive in the mangrove swamps of the Sundarbans.

DELTA EXPANSION

The delta has expanded 250 miles (400 km) seaward in 40 million years.

WORLD'S HIGHEST
WATERFALL

HIDDEN WONDER

Because of its remote
location, this spectacular
waterfall remained
unknown to science until
1933, when it was seen
from the air by American
pilot Jimmie Angel.

OUT OF THE BLUE

ANGEL FALLS

In the Gran Sabana region of Venezuela, the landscape is dominated by dramatic flat-topped mountains called tepuis. One of the biggest is known as Auyán-tepui, meaning the "Devil's Mountain." Tropical rain feeds a river that plunges over its sheer cliff, creating the world's highest uninterrupted waterfall—Angel Falls. The height from which this spectacular waterfall plummets is so great that much of the water is blown away as fine mist long before it cascades through the dense forest at the base of the mountain.

AT A GLANCE

- **LOCATION** Southeastern Venezuela, South America
- **TOTAL HEIGHT** 3,212 ft (979 m)
- **LONGEST DROP** 2,648 ft (807 m)
- **WIDTH AT BASE** 492 ft (150 m)

STATS AND FACTS

Angel Falls are part of Venezuela's dramatic Canaima National Park. More than 60 percent of the park is dominated by spectacular tepuis, including Angel Falls.

RECORD BREAKER

Angel Falls is more than twice the height of the Empire State Building.

LOCAL NAME

Known locally as *Kerepakupai Vená,* meaning "waterfall of the deepest place."

TOTAL HEIGHT

The total height of 3,212 ft (979 m) includes the cascade and rapids at the base of Angel Falls as well as the longest drop.

m	300	600	900	1,200
ft	900	1,800	2,700	3,600

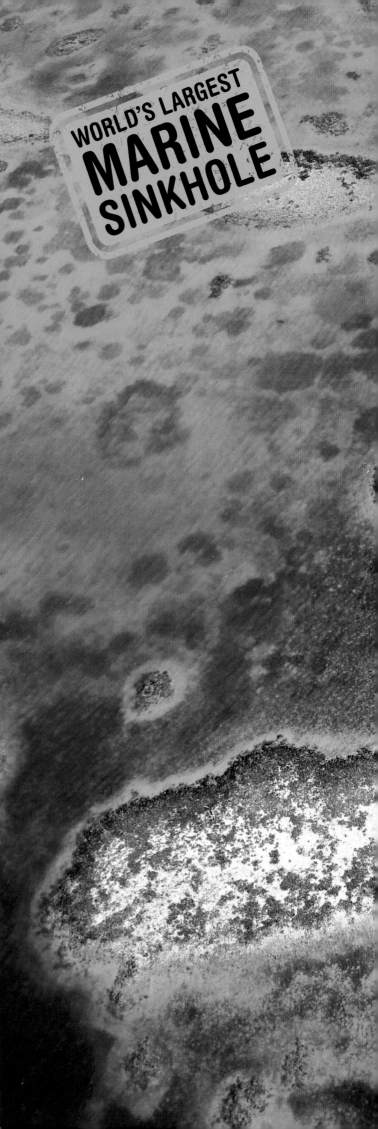

UNDERWATER WONDER
GREAT BLUE HOLE

At the heart of Lighthouse Reef in the Caribbean lies a deep, dark, perfectly circular hole in the seabed. It was formed during the last ice age when the sea level was much lower and the surrounding limestone was dry land. Rainwater seeping into the rock created a limestone cave, and at some point, the roof collapsed to form a circular sinkhole. When the sea level rose at the end of the ice age, seawater flooded in to create the Great Blue Hole.

AT A GLANCE

- **LOCATION** Western Caribbean, 60 miles (80 km) east of central Belize
- **FORMATION** Flooded limestone sinkhole
- **AGE** Formed more than 15,000 years ago
- **STATUS** Part of the Belize Barrier Reef Reserve System, a World Heritage Site

STATS AND FACTS

1,000 FEET (300 M)

WIDTH

The Great Blue Hole is one of the world's most renowned scuba-diving sites.

SINKHOLE CAVE

The cave contains stalactites and stalagmites—typical limestone cave features.

EXPLORATION

The sinkhole was first explored in 1972 by French marine researcher Jacques Cousteau.

TEMPERATURE

The warmest water temperature is about 85°F (29°C).

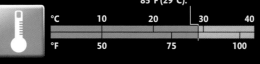

°C		10	20	30	40
°F		50	75	100	

DEPTH

410 FEET (125 M)

DEEP BLUE
The deep water of the Great Blue Hole makes a dramatic contrast with the turquoise glow of the shallow coral reef. In the sinkhole wall, far below the surface, lie flooded limestone caves.

SODA LAKE
LAKE NATRON

Lake Natron is one of the world's most hostile wildlife habitats. It simmers in the scorching heat of Africa's Great Rift Valley. Water flowing into the lake evaporates in the heat, leaving minerals behind that make the remaining water very salty. Volcanic hot springs add more chemicals, creating a caustic alkaline brew of salt and soda that can burn like acid. But amazingly, some forms of life thrive in it, especially vast blooms of a microorganism called *Spirulina*. It attracts flocks of lesser flamingos, which use their especially adapted bills to filter it from the water. The birds eat so much that it tints their feathers pink.

AT A GLANCE

- **LOCATION** Eastern Rift Valley, northern Tanzania, Africa
- **LENGTH** 35 miles (57 km)
- **WIDTH** 14 miles (22 km)
- **SEASON** Lake turns red in the dry season, June–October

STATS AND FACTS

The lake takes its name from natron—a salt deposit (hydrated sodium carbonate) that is left when the lake water evaporates.

ALKALINE LAKE

With a pH level of about 12, the lake's alkalinity is as strong as that of oven cleaners.

PATTERN

Alkali salt deposits form a distinctive criss-cross pattern on the lake.

TEMPERATURE

The water temperature may reach a scalding 140°F (60°C).

°C	20	40	60	80
°F	70	105	140	175

DEPTH

10 FEET (3 M)

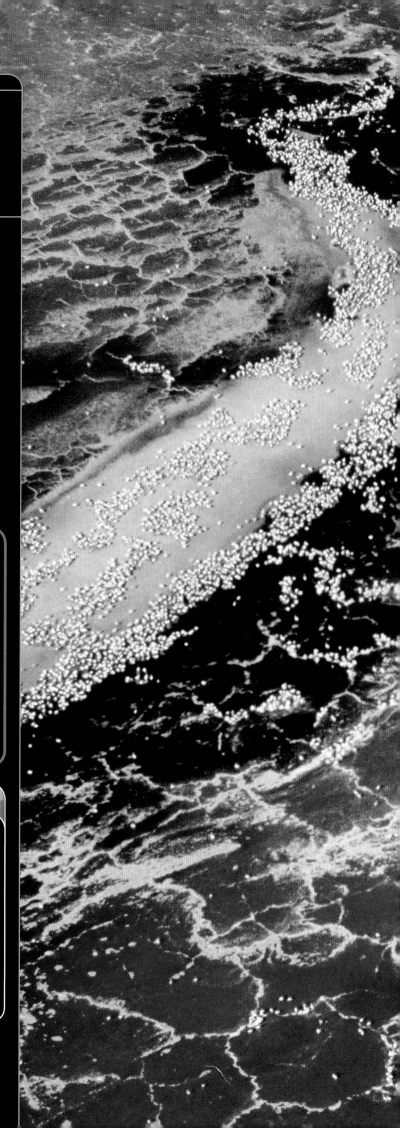

RED ISLAND

Thousands of flamingos gather red *Spirulina* from the soda-crusted water of Lake Natron. Scaly skin protects the birds' legs from the caustic soda. The soda deters predators, and because of this, the lake is the lesser flamingos' main breeding site in Africa.

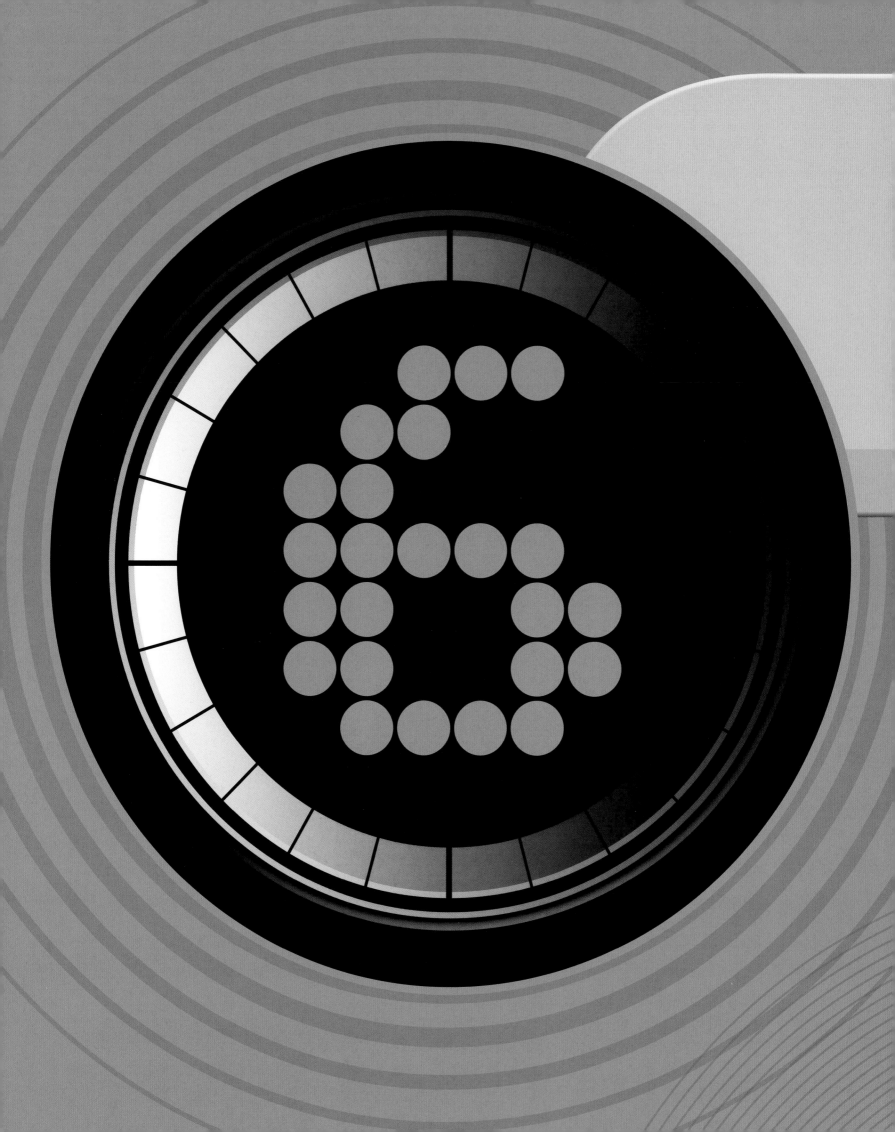

EXTREME WEATHER

Few events demonstrate nature's power more dramatically than a great storm. The destructive energy unleashed by a hurricane or tornado is colossal, while a single storm cloud can contain enough rainwater to drown a city.

SHOCK AND AWE
THUNDERSTORM

Moisture evaporating from warm ground can build gigantic storm clouds. Moist air rising through each cloud generates powerful updrafts that toss water droplets and ice crystals up and down. This produces static electricity in the cloud, charging it like a giant battery. Eventually, the cloud reaches an incredibly high voltage that starts breaking down the electrical resistance of the air, and faint branched leaders of lightning move toward the ground. When one makes contact, the main discharge shoots back up the leader with a much brighter flash—and a loud crack of thunder.

STORM CLOUD

Most clouds are not very deep, and float at different levels. But cumulonimbus storm clouds rise from near the ground all the way to the stratosphere, up to 10 miles (16 km) above ground level. At this height, the cloud cannot build up any higher, and frozen cloud droplets start drifting sideways to create the broad-topped shape typical of thunderclouds.

STATS AND FACTS

Thunderstorms can occur anywhere on Earth, but they are more frequent in the tropics. In cooler climates, they are most common in summer, because they are fuelled by warm air.

ELECTRICAL CHARGE

The electrical charge in a cumulonimbus cloud can exceed 100 million volts.

FREQUENCY

At any given time, about 2,000 thunderstorms occur in different places on Earth.

HEATED AIR

The air along the path of the lightning heats to about 54,000°F (30,000°C).

STORM CLOUD

Thunderstorms caused by just one big cloud usually last less than 30 minutes.

LIGHTNING SPEED

ABOUT
220,000
MPH
(355,000
KM/H)

HIGHEST TEMPERATURE GENERATED ON EARTH

THUNDERBOLT

Lightning flashes in the Arizona Desert as sunlight shining through falling rain creates a rainbow. The intense heat of such a lightning strike can easily spark wildfires in dry terrain.

VOLCANIC LIGHTNING

When tiny, glassy particles of volcanic rock billow from an erupting volcano in a cloud of ash, they rub against each other and generate electricity, just like ice crystals in a storm cloud. The electrical charge can build up until it is released in bolts of lightning, like these flashing from an eruption of Japan's Sakurajima volcano in January 2013.

STORM WARNING
SUPERCELL

The biggest, most powerful thunderstorms are known as supercells. High-altitude wind that is blowing in a different direction from the low-level wind interacts with rising warm, moist air to create a spiral updraft called a mesocyclone. As the moist air rises and cools in the swirling updraft, water vapor condenses to form a gigantic rotating cloud mass that towers high into the sky. The huge cloud often spills torrential rain as well as giant hailstones that can smash glass and cause serious injury. Some supercells also produce intensely destructive tornadoes.

MONSTER HAIL

The powerful updrafts that build storm clouds hurl ice crystals up and down, adding layer upon layer of ice to create hailstones. In supercells, the updrafts are so extreme that they can produce hailstones as large as a human fist. Made of solid, heavy ice, these eventually crash to the ground at high speed, and are very dangerous.

STATS AND FACTS

Giant rotating supercells are especially common in North America, but they can occur anywhere in the world.

SUPERCELL

A supercell may be more than 9 miles (15 km) high.

HAILSTONES

Giant hainstones can be up to 8 in (20 cm) across and weigh 2.2 lb (1 kg).

WIND SPEED

Powerful ground level wind speeds from supercells can reach up to 92 mph (148 km/h).

km/h	112	130	148	166
mph	68	80	92	104

DIAMETER

ABOUT
25
MILES
(40 KM)

LOOMING THREAT

A deluge of rain and hail cascades from a supercell sweeping across the open prairie in Montana. Supercell storms are a regular event on the plains of the American Midwest.

DEADLY TWISTER

TORNADO

A supercell storm can trigger the most terrifying of all weather events—a tornado. This violent, swirling funnel of air extends from the base of a supercell to the ground. It focuses most of the storm's energy in one small area, generating incredibly strong winds. These spin around a center of extremely low air pressure that acts like a giant vacuum hose, sucking up dust and debris and hurling it high in the air. Some tornadoes are powerful enough to rip houses apart, toss heavy trucks upside down, and even derail trains. Anyone caught in the path of such a storm would be very lucky to survive.

TERROR TRAIL

Tornadoes only affect small areas as they travel across the country, but they leave long trails of destruction in their wake, as seen here in Illinois in 2013. Houses that stood in the path of the tornado were completely destroyed, whereas areas on either side of the storm track remained untouched.

STATS AND FACTS

Tornadoes occur throughout the world, including Asia, New Zealand, and South America, but they are most frequent in the prairie states of the American Midwest. Tornadoes that form over water are called waterspouts.

SPINNING POWER

The spinning winds suck up anything in their path and drop the debris several miles away.

TORNADO ALLEY

Every year, about 1,200 tornadoes hit the US, mostly in an area known as Tornado Alley.

WIND SPEED

Wind speeds in a tornado can reach more than 310 mph (500 km/h).

km/h	400	500
mph	250	310

DESTROYER

Shown here is a tornado that was one of at least 14 that tore across the open plains of Colorado on a single day in June 2015. Brown earth and dust were whirled skyward, but the farm buildings survived intact.

GRAND SLAM
MICROBURST

Strong updrafts of warm, moist air build up giant storm clouds. But as the warm air rises through the core of the cloud, cold air sinks through other parts of the cloud where there is no rising airflow. Rain and hail can chill the sinking air even further, making it heavier so that it falls from the sky faster and faster, like an avalanche. This is called a downburst, or microburst. When it slams into the ground, the cold air rushes out from the point of impact at high speed in powerful winds that can cause serious damage. Microbursts can be so violent that they are mistaken for tornadoes.

FLASH FLOOD

Torrential rain cascading out of a huge storm cloud can make rivers and streams burst their banks. The water spills across roads and through towns in surging torrents. These flash floods can carry away bridges, destroy buildings, wreck cars, and force hundreds of people from their homes.

STATS AND FACTS

A microburst is caused by a downdraft of cold air, which forces winds to blow outward. This is the opposite of a tornado, but it can be almost as destructive.

TIMESPAN

A microburst can last from a few seconds to several minutes.

DOWNPOUR

A big storm cloud can release up to 300,000 tons of water in torrential rain.

WIND SPEED

A microburst can generate wind speeds higher than 170 mph (270 km/h).

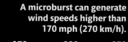

km/h	170	220	270	320
mph	110	140	170	200

DIAMETER

ABOUT
2.5
MILES
(4 KM)

DOWNFALL
Rain, hail, and cold air plunge to the ground in this spectacular microburst over Phoenix, Arizona. Similar microbursts have been known to strike airports and cause the fatal crashes of planes that are landing.

FURIOUS STORM
HURRICANE

In tropical regions close to the equator, huge storms called hurricanes build up over oceans heated by intense sunshine. Warm, moist air rises off the sea, forming gigantic storm clouds. The rising air near the center of the storm drags surrounding air inward in a spiraling hurricane, generating howling winds and huge waves.

Eye of the storm

Air dragged into a hurricane moves faster and faster as it approaches the center, but the eye of the storm is strangely calm. Meanwhile, moisture rising off the warm sea builds towering spiral walls of cloud that are tallest around the eye. A canopy of thin clouds spills out from the tops of the highest clouds, while torrential rain deluges the sea below.

BIGGEST STORMS ON EARTH

High-level cloud spills out in the opposite direction to the low-level cloud spiral.

Outflowing air creates a spiral canopy of thin, icy cirrus cloud.

Air that has risen to the top of the hurricane flows outwards over the storm.

Seawater needs to be at least 200 ft (60 m) deep for a tropical storm to occur.

STATS AND FACTS

Hurricanes form in the tropical Atlantic and eastern Pacific oceans. Similar storms in the Indian Ocean and south Pacific are called tropical cyclones, while in the northwestern Pacific they are called typhoons.

WIND SPEED

Sustained wind speeds can reach 346 km/h (215 mph), strong enough to destroy buildings.

STORM SURGE HEIGHT

A hurricane storm surge can be more than 26 ft (8 m) higher than normal sea level.

HURRICANE SIZE

A hurricane can be up to 2,220 km (1,380 miles) across – nearly half the size of the USA.

DURATION

A hurricane can last up to a month out at sea, traveling relatively slowly at about 15 mph (24 km/h).

HURRICANES PER YEAR
ABOUT
85
WORLDWIDE

Air swirling into the center of the hurricane rises over the warm ocean, building spiral bands of rain cloud.

STORM SURGE

Winds blowing toward the eye of the storm drag ocean water into a heap called a storm surge. Very low air pressure at the center allows the surge to rise even higher. If the hurricane then hits land, the storm surge sweeps ashore like a tsunami. These houses in New Jersey were wrecked by a storm surge caused by Hurricane Sandy in 2012.

At the eye of the storm, there is little wind, and sinking air stops clouds from forming.

Ascending warm air builds the storm clouds, which are similar to those that cause thunderstorms.

The tallest clouds form the eye wall. This zone has the strongest winds and heaviest rain.

Cool, dry air sinks between the spiral cloud bands.

A hurricane can only build up over a tropical ocean with a surface temperature higher than 80°F (27°C).

The surface winds swirl into the storm, getting stronger as they approach the center.

The strong winds build huge waves out at sea, and cause great destruction if the storm moves over land.

HURRICANE MATTHEW

A storm-tracking satellite captured this image of Hurricane Matthew in early October 2016, soon after it intensified into a Category 5 hurricane. The eye of the storm is visible at the center of the spiral of towering rain clouds. On October 4, the hurricane moved north across the island of Haiti, causing massive damage and up to 1,600 deaths before wreaking havoc in the southeastern US.

SHROUDED IN ICE
ICE STORM

Water in the air usually freezes at 32°F (0°C), but it needs something to freeze onto, such as the tiny particles of dust that allow it to form snowflakes. If the air is very pure, airborne water can be chilled to well below its usual freezing point. If this supercooled water then touches something cold, it freezes almost instantly to create thick layers of ice. These ice storms can smother trees, buildings, and even vehicles with enough heavy ice to make them collapse, and they can cause more damage than the howling winds of a hurricane.

FROZEN SOLID

A deep freeze engulfed these cars parked on the shores of Lake Geneva, Switzerland, in 2005. It was caused by water being swept off the lake by very cold winds. Other ice storms are caused by freezing rain—supercooled liquid raindrops that freeze solid when they land on ice-cold surfaces.

STATS AND FACTS

An ice storm is not a violent, windy event. It usually happens silently, at night, as ice slowly builds up into a thick glaze that can paralyze an entire city for many weeks.

ICY HAZARD

Some ice storms only last for hours, enough time to turn trees and cars into ice statues.

POWER SUPPLY

In 1998, an ice storm in Canada left 3 million people without power for up to six weeks.

ICE BUILD UP

Up to 8 in (20 cm) of ice can build up from the accumulation of freezing rain during an ice storm.

cm	5	10	15	20
in	2	4	6	8

ICE HOUSE

Supercooled spray blowing off Lake Michigan, USA, in the winter of 2014 froze onto a lighthouse to create this incredible scene. The water often drips before it freezes, forming spectacular icicles.

FUNNEL OF FLAME
FIRE DEVIL

When wildfires in hot, dry parts of the world burn out of control, the intense heat creates powerful updrafts that suck in air from all around the fire zone. The oxygen in the air makes the fire burn even more fiercely, dragging in more air that starts spiraling up in a whirling funnel of flame called a fire devil. Like a miniature burning tornado, it can leave a trail of destruction and scatter burning debris over a large area, sparking new fires and more fire devils.

FIRESTORM

A really big wildfire can create such a powerful updraft that the smoke and water vapor build up a giant, smoky storm cloud—a pyrocumulonimbus. Such clouds can start spinning, becoming supercells that may develop into tornadoes. Acting like supersized fire devils, these firestorms destroy everything in their path.

STATS AND FACTS

Most fire devils are small, local events that last for just a few minutes. Huge fire devils that turn into catastrophic firestorms and tornadoes can only be generated by massive fires, and are extremely rare.

HEIGHT

Fire devils are usually 7–33 ft (2–10 m) high.

DEADLY FIRE DEVIL

In 1923, a fire tornado in Tokyo, Japan, killed 38,000 people in 15 minutes.

TEMPERATURE

Temperatures inside a fire devil can exceed 1,830°F (1,000°C).

°C		500	1,000
°F		1,000	2,000

LINE OF FIRE
This fire devil spiraled up from a wildfire that swept through southern California in 2016. The fire burned more than 58 sq miles (150 sq km) of land, and destroyed more than 100 homes.

SUPERCHARGED

The glowing green veil of this aurora is created by charged particles in the atmosphere colliding with oxygen about 125 miles (200 km) above the ground. The deep crimson glow is due to the presence of nitrogen particles.

SHIMMERING LIGHT SHOW

AURORA BOREALIS

As night falls over the polar north, the sky is often lit up by shimmering ribbons of vivid color that ripple through the icy air overhead. This spectacular effect is called the Aurora Borealis, or the Northern Lights. The phenomenon occurs when electrically charged particles that stream from the Sun are deflected toward the North Pole by Earth's magnetic field. The particles slam into gas particles in the air, energizing them so that they glow. The color depends on the altitude of the collision and the type of gas.

AURORA AUSTRALIS

Charged particles streaming toward the South Pole create the Aurora Australis (the Southern Lights), seen here from space. Since it occurs above Antarctica, the Aurora Australis is usually seen only from ships on the cold Southern Ocean, but it is sometimes visible from southern New Zealand, Tasmania, and the southernmost tip of South America.

STATS AND FACTS

An aurora often starts with a low, soft green arc, like a green rainbow, that gets brighter and bigger before other colors such as blue, violet, and red appear. It can last for a few minutes or several hours.

BAD OMEN

In the past, auroras that appeared over Europe were seen as bad omens of war or plague.

IN SPACE

Auroras also occur on other planets, such as Jupiter and Saturn.

ALTITUDE

The light show can extend up to 190 miles (300 km) into the atmosphere.

km	100	200	300	400
miles		100	200	

DRENCHED

A farmer in Odisha, eastern India, wheels his crop-laden bicycle through a deluge of warm, but drenching rain. Each year the monsoon clouds build up over Odisha from about mid-June, ending weeks of bone-dry weather and scorching heat.

DELUGE
SOUTH ASIAN MONSOON

Every summer the Indian subcontinent experiences months of heavy rain. At the end of summer the heavy rain stops, and there may be months of drought before rain falls again. The reason for this is a seasonal wind shift called the monsoon. In winter, cold dry air sinks over central Asia and pushes south across India. But as Asia warms up in summer, the warm ground heats the air above so that it rises and draws in warm, moist air from the tropical Indian Ocean. Huge black clouds build up and cause torrential rain across India and nearby countries. The rain is especially heavy because the Sun is directly overhead in summer, and this causes intense evaporation of water from the warm ocean.

FLOODING

Monsoon rain is vital for Asian farmers, and its arrival is often a cause for celebration. But the heavy rain swells rivers and makes them overflow, especially the rivers that flow off the high mountains to the north. This can cause catastrophic flooding in low-lying regions such as Bangladesh.

STATS AND FACTS

The heavy rain and floods of the South Asian monsoon affect many Asian countries, from Pakistan, India, and Bangladesh to Thailand and Vietnam.

WORST HIT

In 1997, 10 million people were left homeless due to a monsoon flood in Bangladesh.

INDIAN MONSOON

The summer monsoon accounts for 80 percent of the rainfall in India.

RAINS

Monsoon rains advance across Asia at a rate of about 62 miles (100 km) per day.

km	50	100	150
miles	31	62	93

CHOKING DUST CLOUD

DUST STORM

In regions with very dry climates, strong winds can pick up fine particles of dry soil, hurling them high in the air in vast, wind-blown dust clouds. In the deserts of Arabia and North Africa, these events are often called sandstorms, but sand grains are too heavy to be lifted very high off the ground; most of the cloud is made of fine dust that blocks out the sunlight. A dust storm can strip soil from the ground, destroying valuable farmland, and if the cloud descends on inhabited places, it can have deadly effects as people choke on the dust-filled air.

LAND OF DUST

In eastern China, an area the size of France is covered with an immense depth of fine yellow sediment called loess. It was blown there by huge dust storms in the distant past, and is the source of frequent dust storms now. It is also carried away by water, and this yellow-tinted water feeds China's Yellow River.

STATS AND FACTS

Dust storms are most frequent in North Africa and Arabia, but they may also occur in Australia, China, and even in the North American prairies.

DUST WALL

The wall of dust created by a dust storm may be up to 1 mile (1.6 km) high.

RISING DUST

Dust can rise to heights of 1.9 miles (3 km), and be blown around the world.

WIND SPEED

Some dust storms involve wind speeds of up to 60 mph (100 km/h).

DUST HAZARD

Some parts of North Africa suffer 80 or more dust storms a year.

DESERT STORM

A huge wall of dust bears down on the city of Kuwait. Such dust storms are a regular event in deserts, where there is little vegetation to hold the soil together and stop it from drying out in the hot climate.

DISASTER ZONES

Every year, many parts
of the world suffer major
storms, fires, volcanic eruptions,
and other natural disasters.
Some cause chaos on a gigantic
scale, destroying entire cities and
inflicting terrible loss of life.

DANGER ZONE
PHILIPPINE EARTHQUAKE

All around the Pacific Ocean, people live under the constant threat of earthquakes caused by the ocean floor grinding beneath nearby continents. Worst hit are regions that lie near the deep ocean trenches, especially in the high-risk earthquake zone, known as the Pacific Ring of Fire. This includes the Philippines, which have suffered more than 25 earthquakes since the year 2000—there were nine earthquakes in 2012 alone. The sudden fracture of the earth generates shock waves that cause chaos, wrecking whole communities and claiming lives.

AT A GLANCE

- **LOCATION** Negros, Philippine islands, Southeast Asia
- **EARTHQUAKE MAGNITUDE** 6.7
- **TYPE** Fault rupture at junction of several tectonic plates
- **DATE** February 6, 2012

STATS AND FACTS

The location of the Philippines on the Pacific Ring of Fire means that they suffer many earthquakes every year. Most of these are just tremors, and some are so small that few people notice them. But every few years, a catastrophic earthquake shakes the region.

AFTERMATH

Although the 2012 earthquake was not the deadliest, it left 23,500 people homeless.

TREMOR DEPTH

The earthquake tremor was 6.8 miles (11 km) below ground.

EARTHQUAKE SCALE

In the Philippines, the strongest recorded earthquake had a magnitude of 8.7.

1-4 Measured but no damage	5-7 Some structural damage	8-10 Extreme destruction

SHATTERED LIVES

A day after an earthquake struck a central Philippine island in February 2012, local people make their way along a road reduced to rubble by the shock. The earthquake caused several deadly landslides.

WAVE OF DEATH
JAPANESE TSUNAMI

On Friday, March 11, 2011, at 2:46 PM, part of the Pacific Ocean floor suddenly slipped at least 66 feet (20 meters) west beneath central Japan, causing a massive earthquake. As the rocks gave way, part of the seabed sprang up by 23 feet (7 meters), pushing up broad, shallow waves that raced across the ocean toward the east coast of Japan. As they swept into shallow water, these waves were slowed down. But this made them pile up into gigantic walls of water that surged ashore in devastating tsunamis. Entire coastal towns were wiped out, and thousands of people died as they were overwhelmed and drowned by the deluge of water and floating debris.

AT A GLANCE

- **LOCATION** Triggered by earthquake in the Japan Trench off Sendai in northern Honshu, Japan

- **EARTHQUAKE MAGNITUDE** 9.0

- **TYPE** Fault rupture at convergent plate boundary

- **AREA FLOODED** 216 sq miles (560 sq km)

STATS AND FACTS

The tsunami was far more destructive than the earthquake that caused it. The waves also traveled across the Pacific, reaching Alaska, Hawaii, Chile, and even Antarctica.

SUDDEN SHIFT

The main island of Japan, Honshu, shifted east by 8 ft (2.4 m) due to the earthquake.

FLOATING DEBRIS

An estimated 5.5 million tons of debris was carried out to sea.

DESTRUCTION

The tsunami waves caused damage up to 128 ft (39 m) above the normal sea level.

UNDERSEA EARTHQUAKE

The sea floor rupture was about 300 miles (500 km) in length.

COASTAL WAVE HEIGHT

UP TO
33
FEET
(10 M)

TOTAL CHAOS

The surge of water carried everything with it—houses, cars, and even ships. Only the strongest concrete buildings were left standing, and most of those were wrecked by the debris that swept over them.

COSTLIEST NATURAL DISASTER

AVALANCHE OF FIRE
POMPEII

Mount Vesuvius in Italy is one of the world's most dangerous volcanoes. This was proved nearly 2,000 years ago, when an explosive eruption hurled a vast cloud of volcanic gas and ash high into the sky. As people ran for their lives, parts of the ash cloud collapsed and surged downhill in high-speed avalanches of lethally hot gas and rock. These pyroclastic flows overwhelmed the nearby cities of Pompeii and Herculaneum, killing thousands of people within seconds, and burying them in deep layers of ash.

AT A GLANCE

- **LOCATION** Near Naples in southern Italy
- **VOLCANO TYPE** Stratovolcano
- **ERUPTION DATE** 79 CE
- **ERUPTION TYPE** Explosive, with pyroclastic flows

STATS AND FACTS

Traces of about 1,500 people buried by the eruption have been found in Pompeii. Their bodies left cavities in the ash, which excavators have used as moulds to create plaster casts.

MOUNT VESUVIUS

Since 79 CE, Mount Vesuvius has erupted about 36 times.

BURIED IN ASH

Animals were buried in ash, too, including a dog guarding the house of its owner.

TEMPERATURE

The pyroclastic flows of hot gas and rock had a temperature of up to 572°F (300°C).

°C	100	200	300
°F	212	392	572

ASH CLOUD WAS

UP TO
19
MILES
(30 KM)
HIGH

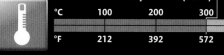

DARK THREAT

The cratered peak of Mount Vesuvius looms over the shattered ruins of Pompeii, excavated from volcanic ash 80 ft (25 m) deep. The entire city was destroyed, along with most of its citizens by the eruption. If the volcano erupts again, the modern city of Naples could suffer the same fate.

BIG BANG
MOUNT PINATUBO

Some volcanoes erupt with frequent displays of smoke and fire; others lie dormant, building up pressure over centuries before detonating in highly destructive explosions, like Mount Pinatubo in the Philippines. In 1991, after a 600-year silence, this volcano shook the islands with a series of eruptions that blasted a huge cloud of ash and gas high into the atmosphere. Sulfur dioxide gas combined with water in the air to create vast quantities of sulfuric acid. This swept around the globe in an acid haze that dimmed the Sun for more than two years. Meanwhile, ash settling around the volcano smothered the landscape in a ghostly shroud of white.

AT A GLANCE

- **LOCATION** Luzon, Philippines
- **VOLCANO TYPE** Stratovolcano
- **ERUPTION TYPE** Explosive, ultra-plinian
- **ASH VOLUME ERUPTED** At least 2.4 cubic miles (10 cubic km)

STATS AND FACTS

The 1991 Mount Pinatubo eruption was the most destructive eruption since Krakatoa in the Dutch East Indies (now Indonesia) in 1883. An estimated 847 people were killed, fewer than might be expected, thanks to the evacuation of 20,000 people living in the area.

EXPLOSIVE ERUPTION

The eruption was ten times larger than the 1980 eruption of Mt St Helens.

GLOBAL EFFECT

The acid haze reduced sunlight levels, lowering temperatures by 1°F (0.5°C).

ASH CLOUD

The cloud of volcanic ash was up to 21 miles (34 km) high.

km	10	20	30	40
miles		10	20	

DEADLY CLOUD

Avalanches of searing hot ash and gas cascaded down the flanks of the volcano, filling river valleys and threatening to overwhelm these people fleeing for their lives. Miraculously, they managed to escape.

Before the catastrophic eruption of 1991, Mount Pinatubo was a rugged peak covered by dense rainforest. The eruption emptied the magma chamber beneath the volcano, making most of the peak collapse into the void below. This formed a giant crater—a caldera—which soon filled with water to create Lake Pinatubo.

INFERNO

At the peak of the fire, flames were leaping 330 ft (100 m) into the air. The heat was so intense that trees burst into flames before the fire reached them. The fire service was overwhelmed by the inferno.

FIRESTORM
BLACK SATURDAY BUSHFIRES

Every year, wildfires sweep through dry woodlands. These are a natural part of the ecology, but some can become raging infernos. On Saturday, February 7, 2009, very hot, dry, windy conditions in the Australian state of Victoria sparked a series of huge fires that burned out of control for days. In one area near Melbourne, the intense heat created powerful updrafts that sucked in more air, fueling deadly firestorms. They reduced whole towns to ashes. Thousands of homes were destroyed, and many people died in the flames.

AT A GLANCE

- **LOCATION** Victoria, southeastern Australia
- **SEASON** High summer
- **CAUSE** Record heat and very low humidity, plus strong winds
- **NUMBER OF FIRES** At least 400

STATS AND FACTS

Wildfires occur all over the world, but the Black Saturday bushfires were particularly destructive—about 1,740 sq miles (4,500 sq km) of landscape was burned.

FIREFIGHTING

About 5,000 firefighters tackled the deadly fire.

DESTRUCTION

More than 2,000 houses were destroyed by the flames.

DEADLY HEAT

In places, the heat was enough to kill anyone within 980 ft (300 m).

m	100	200	300	400
ft	300	600	900	1,200

LEFT HOMELESS

7,562 PEOPLE

STORM SURGE
HURRICANE KATRINA

Every summer, hurricanes build up in the tropical North Atlantic and sweep west toward America. In August 2005, the fifth hurricane of the season—Hurricane Katrina—veered north over the Gulf of Mexico and headed directly for the region's largest city, New Orleans. The strength of the storm had pushed up a great mound of ocean water, creating a storm surge that was up to 28 feet (8.5 meters) higher than normal sea level. Topped by huge waves swept onshore by the screaming winds, it broke through the sea defenses like a tsunami. Most of the low-lying city was flooded, whole neighborhoods were reduced to ruins, and hundreds of people drowned.

AT A GLANCE

- **LOCATION** New Orleans, Louisiana
- **DATE** August 29–30, 2005
- **HURRICANE FORCE** Category 5, weakening to Category 3 at landfall
- **WIND SPEED** More than 125 mph (200 km/h)

STATS AND FACTS

Katrina was one of the five deadliest hurricanes in the history of the US. At least two-thirds of the casualties were victims of the flooding caused by the storm surge.

WIND SPEED

The highest recorded wind speed was 175 mph (280 km/h).

INLAND WATER

Water was swept up to 12 miles (20 km) inland.

FLOOD DEPTH

Eighty percent of New Orleans was flooded, in places to depths of 20 ft (6 m) or more.

m	2	4	6
ft	10		20

ECONOMIC COST
108
BILLION DOLLARS

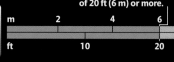

UNDERWATER CITY

In the calm after the storm, New Orleans is transformed into a giant lake. More than a million people were left homeless, while five million were left without power.

DROUGHT AND FAMINE

SAHEL DROUGHT

Many tropical countries have alternating dry and rainy seasons, so people rely on crops that they can grow in the months when it rains. But sometimes the rain does not fall, the land turns to dust, and the crops fail. The worst of these droughts have occurred in the Sahel region on the southern fringes of the Sahara Desert in Africa. Some droughts have lasted many years, and as water supplies dry up and crops wither in the fields, farm animals die and the people starve. Such famines may occur more frequently, as climate change makes the seasonal rains even less dependable.

AT A GLANCE

- **LOCATION** South of the Sahara, from the Atlantic to the Red Sea
- **AREA** 1,158,000 sq miles (3 million sq km)
- **POPULATION AT RISK** 15 million
- **LONGEST RECENT DROUGHT** From 1968 to 1974

STATS AND FACTS

Droughts can occur almost anywhere in the world, but they are most severe in the poorer nations of the tropics, where people are at risk of famine. They are often forced to rely on humanitarian aid for survival.

DISASTER

A drought from the 1960s–80s affected most of the 50 million people living in the Sahel.

RAINFALL

There is less than than 4 in (10 cm) of rainfall a year in the Sahel region.

TEMPERATURE

Temperature is a key drought factor. On June 25, 2010, it peaked at 121.3°F (49.6°C) in the Sudan, eastern Sahel.

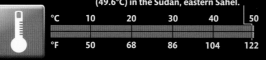

°C	10	20	30	40	50
°F	50	68	86	104	122

DRY AS DUST

This expanse of baked mud was once a lake, but months of drought have reduced it to an arid waste. There may be water deep below ground, but if the rain does not fall the land could turn to desert.

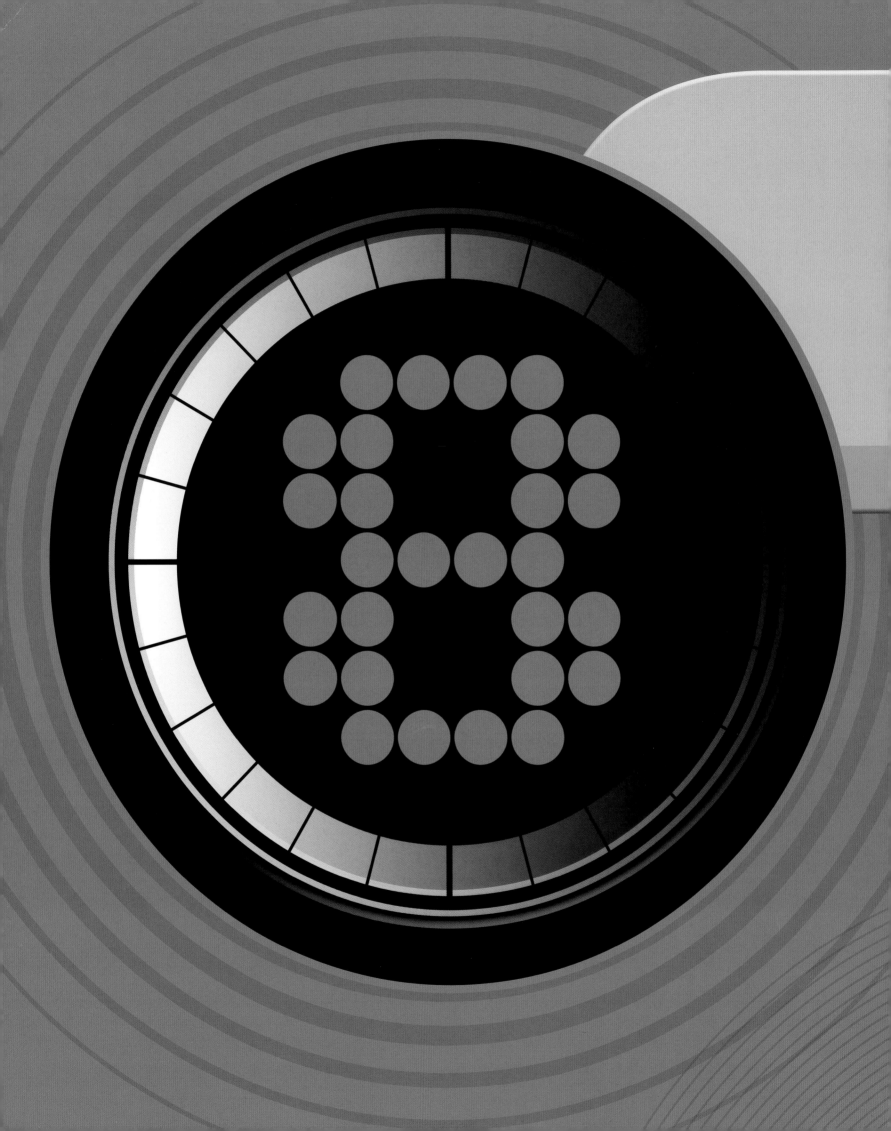

LIVING EARTH

Earth is the only planet in our solar system that can support life. Its oceans and continents swarm with a great variety of living things—from microscopic bacteria to giant whales and towering trees. Each part of this world is home to a unique mix of animals and plants that have adapted to life in their specific habitat.

LUXURIANT LIFE

Mist rises off lush lowland rainforest in Borneo as the leaves pump out moisture in the morning sunshine. Much of the mist will form clouds and rain later in the day so, to some extent, the rainforest creates its own climate.

RICHEST LAND HABITAT

LIVING PARADISE
RAINFOREST

Tropical rainforests are the richest wildlife habitats, supporting an astonishing diversity of plants and animals, all in vast numbers. These forests thrive in an ideal climate of constant warmth and daily rain. This allows trees and other plants to keep growing, flowering, and fruiting all through the year, so the forest animals never go short of food. Many animals spend most of their lives in the tree canopy, including troops of monkeys that travel through the treetops in search of fruiting trees, insect-eating tree frogs, and leaf-eating sloths. Even small plants such as orchids cling to branches, soaking up the sunlight high above the dark forest floor.

AROUND THE WORLD

Tropical rainforests are found around the equator. They cover only 6 percent of the planet but are home to more than half the world's plant and animal life. The largest tropical rainforest on Earth lies in the Amazon basin of South America, extending north into Central America.

FOREST LAYERS

A rainforest is a multi-story living space with four distinct levels. The forest floor gets very little light and supports a sparse ground layer of plants, allowing big animals to move around easily. An understory of taller plants grows beneath the main tree canopy. The tallest emergent trees rise above the canopy.

- ■ EMERGENT TREES
- ■ CANOPY
- ■ UNDERSTORY
- ■ GROUND LAYER

LIFE ON THE PLAINS

The broad grasslands of the Serengeti in East Africa are dotted with tall acacia trees, which are well equipped to survive the droughts of the tropical dry season. Their foliage is a favorite food of the African elephants that roam the grassy plains.

TROPICAL GRASSLAND
SAVANNA

Many tropical regions are too dry to allow the growth of dense forests, and instead they develop into grassy savannas. Some have a lot of trees, but drier savannas are seas of grass with just a few scattered trees. In Africa, these grasslands support huge herds of grazing animals. The grass withers and often burns in the tropical dry season, forcing the animals to migrate in search of food. But the return of the rainy season makes the grass sprout again, and the grazing herds return.

AROUND THE WORLD

Savanna grasslands occur in the tropics, close to the equator but away from the high-rainfall zones that support tropical rainforests. These grassy plains with scattered, drought-resistant trees such as acacia and baobab are most extensive in Africa, but savannas also occur in South America, parts of India, and northern Australia.

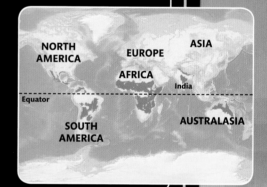

NORTH AMERICA · EUROPE · ASIA · AFRICA · India · Equator · SOUTH AMERICA · AUSTRALASIA

NO HIDING PLACE

The animals that graze the African savannas are hunted by powerful predators such as this lion. Since there is nowhere to hide on the open plains, most of the grazing animals have evolved the ability to run fast to escape their enemies. But many hunters can also run fast, and they may also use stealth tactics to creep up on their prey and spring a surprise attack.

SPINY STORAGE

Tall saguaro cacti dominate this desert scene in Arizona. The pleats in their spiny stems let them expand to store as much water as possible. Smaller cacti and woody shrubs grow nearby.

DROUGHT SURVIVORS
DESERT

Regions that get very little rain become deserts. Their clear skies allow the Sun to shine all day, so most deserts are very hot, although they cool down at night. This is a harsh environment for plant life, so the driest deserts are virtually barren. But others get some rain, and plants have evolved ways of making the most of it. Thorny shrubs have long roots for soaking it up and small leaves to reduce water loss. The cacti of American deserts have fleshy stems that store water, and other plants have fleshy roots for the same job. Some plants survive for years as seeds; they sprout, flower, and produce seeds only if they are soaked by a rare rainstorm.

AROUND THE WORLD

Most deserts lie in the world's subtropics, where high-level air moving away from the equator sinks and stops the formation of clouds. Cold central Asian deserts are cut off from rain-bearing oceanic air by high mountain ranges such as the Himalayas.

NIGHT HUNTER

Insects, lizards, and small burrowing mammals such as mice are often common in deserts. Most of them hide underground by day, and emerge to feed at night. They provide prey for hunters like this American elf owl, which often nests in holes bored in big cacti by woodpeckers.

LIVING EARTH

195

SEASONAL RICHES

TEMPERATE FOREST

Between the tropics and the icy polar regions lie parts of the world that have warm summers, mild but frosty winters, and regular rain. Where there is enough rain for trees to grow well, the natural vegetation is temperate forest. Some of the trees in these regions are evergreen, with small, tough leaves that can survive freezing in winter. But most have broader, thinner leaves that fall from the trees in autumn, leaving bare twigs. These deciduous trees stay dormant all winter and grow new leaves in spring. The fresh leaves are more efficient at soaking up sunlight than tough evergreen ones, and this enables them to make all the food the trees need to grow and reproduce.

AROUND THE WORLD

Temperate deciduous forests are found in the eastern US, western Europe, and eastern Asia. Similar regions that do not suffer frosty winters develop evergreen temperate rainforests. They include parts of the western USA, southern South America, Australia, and New Zealand.

SUMMER VISITOR

When new leaves appear on the trees in spring, this triggers a mass hatching of leaf-eating insects. These attract migrant birds such as this European redstart, which flies north from the tropics to nest and feed its young on the insects. In autumn, the birds fly back to Africa.

AUTUMNAL COLOR

As winter approaches in England, deciduous trees absorb and recycle the green pigments in their leaves. This makes the leaves change color to brown, yellow, or red before they fall to the ground.

WINTER CHILL
BOREAL FOREST

Between the northern temperate regions and the icy Arctic lies the boreal forest zone—a huge swath of mainly evergreen trees. Also known as the taiga forest, it survives some of the lowest temperatures on Earth outside Antarctica. Most of the trees are conifers such as spruces and pines. They have tough needle-shaped leaves that can withstand freezing, and are always ready to soak up the energy of the Sun whenever it shines. Beneath the trees, the ground is often waterlogged and boggy with streams and pools that freeze over in winter.

AROUND THE WORLD

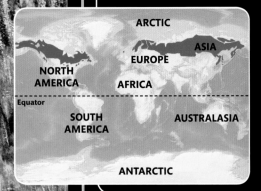

ARCTIC

ASIA

EUROPE

NORTH AMERICA

AFRICA

Equator

SOUTH AMERICA

AUSTRALASIA

ANTARCTIC

The Boreal forest, or taiga, spans most of Scandinavia, Russia, Siberia, Alaska, and Canada. At its northern fringes, the trees give way to Arctic tundra. There is no boreal forest in the Southern Hemisphere because there is very little land at the right latitude between the equator and Antarctica.

ICY DEFENSES

The animals that live in the boreal forest have to be tough to survive the harsh winters. Beavers survive by storing food in ponds. These freeze over, which keeps the food fresh. The beavers dam streams to make the ponds deeper and build their homes in the middle, where they are safe from predators such as wolves. When the water freezes over, the beavers stay hidden beneath the ice

WINTER TREES

Dark conifer trees stretch to the horizon in the vast boreal forest of the West Siberian Plain in Russia. Frozen, snow-covered rivers and oxbow lakes loop through the trees, while the low winter Sun casts long shadows.

WORLD'S LARGEST FOREST

SUMMER BLOOM

Low-growing plants bloom on the tundra in Iceland, glowing in the low northern sunlight. Many tundra plants form dense, mossy cushions that can resist freezing winds loaded with ice crystals.

POLAR FRINGE
TUNDRA

The ice sheets of the Arctic and Antarctic are fringed by bleak, almost treeless tundra. In this region, the Sun barely rises above the horizon in winter, so temperatures plummet and any water in the ground freezes. But when summer arrives, it brings almost constant daylight, warming the ground. The surface layers thaw out and often turn the ground into waterlogged swamps. Tough flowering plants that can survive the winter now bloom and set their seeds, while swarming insects breed in the swamp pools. These plants and insects attract summer visitors such as geese, which nest and raise their young, then fly away to warmer regions as the winter snow starts to fall again.

AROUND THE WORLD

Most of the world's tundra lies to the north of the great boreal forests, all around the Arctic Ocean in Alaska, Canada, coastal Greenland, Iceland, Scandinavia, and Russia. It is scattered in the Southern Hemisphere, occurring on the fringes of Antarctica and the remote, rocky islands of the icy Southern Ocean.

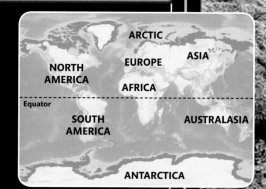

WINTER PROWLER

Many animals only visit the tundra in summer, but a few stay throughout the bitterly cold winter. In the north, they include mouselike lemmings that live under the snow, safe from the freezing winds. They are hunted by predators like this Arctic fox, which is kept warm by its thick white winter fur. Other northern tundra hunters include Arctic wolves and snowy owls.

LIVING EARTH

BENEATH THE WAVES
MARINE HABITATS

BIGGEST **BIOME** ON EARTH

Most life on planet Earth inhabits the oceans. Together, these oceans form a vast living space with many different habitats, ranging from icy polar seas to tropical coral reefs. Nearly all the food in the oceans is tiny algae that drift near the sunlit surface as plankton. All other oceanic life depends on it, and where mineral-rich water fuels a dense growth of plankton, vast shoals of shrimplike animals and small fish are also supported. These are preyed on in turn by bigger fish as well as whales, dolphins, seabirds, and other hunters.

AROUND THE WORLD

ARCTIC OCEAN

ATLANTIC OCEAN

PACIFIC OCEAN

Equator

PACIFIC OCEAN

INDIAN OCEAN

SOUTHERN OCEAN

The world's oceans cover more than two-thirds of the planet, and have an average depth of 12,470 ft (3,800 m). Most oceanic animals live in the sunlit zone near the surface, and in shallow coastal seas where there is plenty of food. But there is life everywhere in the oceans, even in the dark depths.

FROZEN OCEANS

In the Arctic and Antarctic, low air temperatures make the oceans freeze over in winter. But fish and other animals flourish beneath the ice, and are hunted by predators such as seals and penguins. In the Arctic, seals are the main prey of polar bears, which hunt on the sea ice all winter long, and rarely return to land.

HIGH-SPEED HUNTER

A big sardine shoal feeding on plankton in the Caribbean Sea has attracted a sailfish—one of the fastest ocean hunters. The shoal scatters as the sailfish attacks, but the hunter will be too quick for many of these fish.

GLOSSARY

ALGAE
Plant-like organisms that use solar energy to make food.

ASTEROID
A relatively small, irregular rocky object orbiting the Sun.

ATMOSPHERE
The layers of gas that surround a planet, retained by gravity.

BACTERIA
Microscopic organisms with a simple single-celled form, and no distinct internal structures.

BASALT
A dark, heavy igneous rock that forms oceanic crust, and erupts as molten lava from oceanic volcanoes.

BEDROCK
The solid rock that lies beneath more recent, softer sediments.

BIOME
One of the major wildlife habitats of the world—for example, rainforest is a biome.

BLACK SMOKER
A hot spring containing dark minerals that erupts from the ocean floor.

CALDERA
A giant crater formed when a volcano collapses into its emptied magma chamber after an eruption.

CANYON
A rocky valley with steep sides.

CAUSTIC
Able to burn by chemical action.

CINDER CONE
A small volcanic cone formed around a volcanic vent, usually on the side of a larger volcano.

COMET
A space object made of ice and dust that travels from the outer solar system and passes around the Sun.

COMPOUND
A substance made of two or more elements. Water is a compound of hydrogen and oxygen.

CONTINENT
A thick slab of relatively light rock that floats on the heavier rock of Earth's mantle.

CONTINENTAL SHELF
The submerged fringe of a continent, forming the relatively shallow floor of a coastal sea.

CONVECTION CURRENTS
Circulating currents in gases, liquids, or even hot, mobile rock, driven by temperature differences.

CORALS
Marine animals that may have a hard base made of limestone. Many live in large groups or colonies that build coral reefs.

CORE
The innermost layer of Earth.

CRUST
The cool, rocky outer shell of Earth.

CRYSTAL
A solid with an orderly internal atomic structure that sometimes shows geometric forms with flat faces.

CUMULONIMBUS
A very deep cloud that rises through all cloud levels, and produces heavy rain, lightning, and hail.

CYCLONE
A weather system of clouds, rain, and strong winds caused by air swirling into a region of warm, moist, rising air.

ELEMENT
A substance that is made up of just one type of atom.

EROSION
Wearing away, usually of rock, by natural forces, such as flowing water.

FAULT
A fracture in Earth's crust, where one slab of rock slides past another.

FISSURE
A deep, narrow gap, such as between rocks.

FLASH FLOOD
A sudden flood caused by heavy rain, which may become a powerful torrent.

FOSSIL
The remains or traces of a living thing that survive the normal processes of decay, and may be turned to stone.

FUMAROLE
An eruption of steam, created from groundwater heated by hot rock.

GALAXY
A circulating system of stars in space.

GEOTHERMAL
Heat below ground, especially where hot springs are created.

GEYSER
A jet of hot water and steam that erupts from volcanically heated rocks.

GLACIATED VALLEY
A valley enlarged and reshaped by flowing glacier ice.

GLACIER
A mass of ice made of compacted snow that flows slowly downhill.

GRANITE
One of the main igneous rocks found in continental crust.

GRAVITY
The force that attracts one object to another and prevents things from floating into space.

GROUNDWATER
Water that lies or flows beneath the ground surface.

GUYOT
A volcanic island that has eroded and subsided beneath the waves, producing a flat-topped underwater feature.

HOTSPOT
A zone of volcanic activity caused by a stationary plume of heat beneath Earth's crust.

ICE AGE
A cold period during Earth's geological history when ice sheets and glaciers advance.

ICEBERG
Part of a glacier or ice shelf that has broken off and floated out to sea.

ICE SHEET
A very large, deep covering of ice over a continent.

ICE SHELF
Part of an ice sheet that extends out from the land and floats on the sea.

IGNEOUS ROCK
A rock formed by the cooling of molten magma or volcanic lava.

LAGOON
An area of shallow water that has been cut off from the sea.

LAVA
Molten rock that erupts from a volcano.

LAVA BOMB
A blob of lava hurled through the air during a volcanic eruption.

LIMESTONE
A sedimentary rock made of calcite that can be dissolved by rainwater.

MAGMA
Molten rock that lies within or beneath Earth's crust.

MAGMA CHAMBER
A reservoir of magma within or below a volcano.

MANGROVE
A type of tree that grows on tropical tidal seashores.

MANTLE
The deep layer of hot rock that lies between Earth's crust and the core.

MANTLE PLUME
An extra-hot region of the mantle that flows slowly upward to form a hotspot beneath the crust.

MEANDER
A natural loop in a river created by the way the banks are built up on one side and eroded on the other.

METAMORPHIC ROCK
A rock that has been transformed by a geological process involving heat, intense pressure, or both.

MID-OCEAN RIDGE
A submarine mountain chain created by volcanoes erupting from a rift in the ocean floor.

MIGRANT
An animal that regularly moves from one region to another, and back again.

MILKY WAY
The galaxy of stars that contains the Sun and our solar system.

MINERAL
A natural solid that usually forms crystals. Rocks are made of minerals.

MOON
A small rocky world that orbits a planet.

MORAINE
A mass of rock debris carried by a glacier, or piled up at its sides or end.

MUDPOT
A type of hot spring created by acid water reducing rock to liquid mud.

NITROGEN
The gas that forms 78 percent of Earth's atmosphere.

NUCLEAR ENERGY
Energy released by the decay of radioactive elements, or by the fusion or splitting of atomic nuclei.

NUTRIENTS
Food substances that are necessary for life and growth.

ORBIT
To circle a planet or star. For example, Earth orbits the Sun, and the Moon orbits Earth.

OXBOW LAKE
A river meander cut off from the main flow, forming a U-shaped lake.

OXIDE
A chemical containing oxygen and one other element, such as a metal.

OXYGEN
The gas that forms 20 percent of Earth's atmosphere, and is vital to life.

PLANKTON
Organisms that drift in water.

PLATEAU
A level area of land that lies at high altitude.

PREDATOR
An animal that kills other animals for food.

PYROCLASTIC FLOW
An avalanche of very hot rock and dust that cascades down the flank of an erupting volcano.

RIFT
A crack in Earth's crust caused by tectonic plates pulling apart.

RIFT VALLEY
A region where part of Earth's crust has dropped into the gap formed by the crust pulling apart.

SALT FLAT
A large expanse of salt, usually formed in a dried-out lake bed.

SANDSTONE
A rock made of sand grains cemented together by other minerals.

SEAMOUNT
An ocean-floor volcano, active or extinct, that is not high enough to form an island.

SEDIMENTARY ROCK
Rock formed from compressed and hardened sediments.

SEDIMENTS
Solid particles such as sand or mud that settle in a layer in rivers or the sea.

SHIELD VOLCANO
A broad volcano built up from layers of fast-flowing basalt lava.

SILT
Fine particles carried by water.

SOLAR SYSTEM
The system of planets, moons, and asteroids orbiting the Sun.

STORM SURGE
A local rise in sea level caused by a storm, such as a hurricane.

STRATOVOLCANO
A conical volcano built up from layers of volcanic ash and slow-flowing lava.

SUBDUCTION ZONE
Where one plate of Earth's crust is diving beneath another, usually creating an ocean trench.

SULFUR
A yellow element, common in rocks and often erupted from volcanoes.

SUPERCELL
A huge storm cloud with a rotating core that may generate a tornado.

SUPERCOOLED
Describes a liquid that is cooled to below its normal freezing point.

SUPERHEATED
Describes a liquid heated under pressure so its temperature rises above its normal boiling point.

SUPERVOLCANO
A gigantic volcano.

TECTONIC PLATE
One of the giant slabs of rock that form Earth's crust. They move slowly across Earth's surface.

TEMPERATE
A climate that is neither very hot nor very cold.

THRUST FAULT
A major fracture in the rocks of Earth's crust where one section is pushed above another.

TRANSFORM FAULT
A boundary between two slabs of Earth's crust where they slide sideways relative to each other.

TRAVERTINE
A type of limestone deposited by the water of hot springs.

TROPICAL
Describes the hot regions to the north and south of the equator.

TSUNAMI
A giant oceanic wave, often generated by an earthquake on the ocean floor.

UNIVERSE
The entirety of space.

VOLATILE
Generally, prone to unpredictable change. Technically, describes a liquid that evaporates at low temperatures.

VOLCANIC ASH
Solid particles formed from lava blown into the air.

VOLCANIC GAS
Gas erupted from volcanoes.

WATER VAPOR
An invisible gas formed when water evaporates into the air.

WEATHERING
The breaking down of rocks and minerals by rain, sunlight, ice, and other climatic effects.

Abbreviations used in this book	
/	per—for example, km/h means kilometers per hour
°C	degrees Celsius
cm	centimeter
°F	degrees Fahrenheit
ft	foot
in	inch
kg	kilogram
km	kilometer
lb	pound
m	meter
mm	millimeter
mph	miles per hour
Mt	Mount
sq	square

INDEX

ACKNOWLEDGMENTS

Dorling Kindersley would like to thank Dr. Michelle Harris, Professor Chris Morley, Professor Antony Morris, Professor Robin Lacassin, and Professor Mark Saunders for expert advice; NASA for the Mount Etna topography data; British Antarctic Survey for the Antarctic topography data; Gary Hanna and Peter Bull for additional illustrations; Jane Thomas and Smiljka Surla for additional design assistance; Jane Evans for proofreading; Carron Brown for the index; Antara Moitra for editorial assistance; Chhaya Sajwan, Neha Sharma, Roshni Kapur, and Vaishali Kalra for design assistance; and Ashwin Raju Adimari for additional picture research.

Picture Credits
The publisher would like to thank the following for their kind permission to reproduce their photographs:

(Key: a-above; b-below/bottom; c-center; f-far; l-left; r-right; t-top)

5 Dreamstime.com: Dirk Sigmund (tc). **Getty Images:** Jim Sugar (tr). **Imagelibrary India Pvt Ltd:** Krzysztof Hanusiak (tl). **6-7 Rex Shutterstock:** Fernando Famiani. **11 NASA:** Johns Hopkins University Applied Physics Laboratory / Southwest Research Institute (c). **12-13 NASA:** JSC. **14 123RF.com:** Boris Stromar / astrobobo (bl). **15 Alamy Stock Photo:** Stocktrek Images, Inc. (cra). **Getty Images:** Marisa López Estivill (crb); Marc Ward / Stocktrek Images (cr). **17 iStockphoto.com:** mafra13 (tr). **18 NOAA PMEL Earth-Ocean Interactions Program:** (bl). **19 Alamy Stock Photo:** Dirk Bleyer / imageBROKER (tl). **Getty Images:** Planet Observer (cra). **NOAA:** NSF (cr). **20 Alamy Stock Photo:** World History Archive (br). **Science Photo Library:** NASA (cr). **21 Alamy Stock Photo:** Stocktrek Images, Inc. (tr). **22-23 Getty Images:** Arctic-Images / Corbis Documentary. **24 Getty Images:** Alex Ogle / AFP (crb); Anthony Asael / Art in All of Us (clb); The Asahi Shimbun (cb). **25 Alamy Stock Photo:** Design Pics Inc (bl). **26 Getty Images:** Guiziou Franck / hemis.fr (br). **27 Alamy Stock Photo:** Arctic Images / Ragnar Th Sigurdsson (bl). **Getty Images:** Kevin Schafer (tl). **NASA:** (br). **U.S. Geological Survey:** Lyn Topinko (cra). **28 Alamy Stock Photo:** Arctic Images / Ragnar Th Sigurdsson (clb). **29 Alamy Stock Photo:** Cultura RM / Art Wolfe (tr); Minden Pictures (cra). **Dreamstime.com:** Hel080808 (crb). **30-31 Getty Images:** Marco Simoni (br). **naturepl.com:** Guy Edwardes. **32 Alamy Stock Photo:** Matthijs Wetterauw (clb). **33 Alamy Stock Photo:** Roland Bouvier (tl); RGB Ventures / SuperStock (cra); Siim Sepp (cb). **Dorling Kindersley:**

Colin Keates / Natural History Museum, London (ca). **Dreamstime.com:** Uhg1234 (cr). **Getty Images:** Andreas Strauss / LOOK-foto (crb). **36 Alamy Stock Photo:** David Noton Photography (clb). **38-39 Jakub Polomski Photography. 40-41 Alamy Stock Photo:** Aurora Photos / Peter Essick. **41 Science Photo Library:** Bernhard Edmaier (crb). **42-43 Getty Images:** Michael Dunning. **42 Getty Images:** JTB Photo (clb). **44-45 Getty Images:** Feng Wei Photography. **44 Getty Images:** Danita Delimont (clb). **46-47 Alamy Stock Photo:** Geoffrey Morgan. **47 Getty Images:** Hermes Images / AGF / UIG (crb). **48-49 Getty Images:** Travelpix Ltd. **48 Dreamstime.com:** Ocskay Bence (cl). **50 Getty Images:** Joe Klamar (br). **51 Alamy Stock Photo:** Tom Bean (tr). **52-53 123RF.com:** Alexander Garaev. **54-55 Alamy Stock Photo:** imageBROKER / Florian Kopp. **54 Alamy Stock Photo:** Pulsar Images (bl). **56-57 Alamy Stock Photo:** age fotostock / M&G Therin-Weise. **57 Alamy Stock Photo:** age fotostock / M&G Therin-Weise (cr). **58-59 Getty Images:** Steve Allen. **59 iStockphoto.com:** skouatroulio (cr). **60-61 Alamy Stock Photo:** Minden Pictures. **61 Getty Images:** Sylvester Adams (crb). **62-63 Getty Images:** Yann Arthus-Bertrand. **63 National Geographic Creative:** Stephen Alvarez (cr). **64 Alamy Stock Photo:** John Warburton-Lee Photography (bl). **66-67 Getty Images:** Nigel Pavitt. **68-69 Getty Images:** Martin Harvey. **68 Getty Images:** Ch'ien Lee / Minden Pictures (clb). **70-71 Getty Images:** Eddie Lluisma. **70 Alamy Stock Photo:** Minden Pictures (cl). **74-75 naturepl.com:** Doug Perrine. **74 Getty Images:** Jim Sugar (cl). **76-77 Dreamstime.com:** Gardendreamer. **78 NASA:** Jeff Schmaltz, LANCE / EOSDIS MODIS Rapid Response Team (clb). **80-81 Getty Images:** Barcroft Media / Barcroft Images / Joel Santos. **80 Getty Images:** Michael Poliza (bl). **82-83 Dreamstime.com:** Dirk Sigmund. **82 iStockphoto.com:** guenterguni (cl). **84-85 Getty Images:** Heath Korvola. **84 Dreamstime.com:** Jan Mika (clb). **86 Science Photo Library:** B. Murton / Southampton Oceanography Centre (tl). **87 imagequestmarine.com:** (cla). **88-89 Getty Images:** Martin Yon. **88 Getty Images:** Planet Observer (clb). **90 Dreamstime.com:** Ollirg (cl). **91 Getty Images:** Tom Pfeiffer / VolcanoDiscovery (cra). **92-93 Science Photo Library:** Bernard Edmaier. **94 Alamy Stock Photo:** D. Hurst (tl). **96-97 Getty Images:** Danita Delimont. **100-101 Dreamstime.com:** Davidrh. **100 Getty Images:** Chlaus Lotscher (clb). **102-103 Getty Images:** Tom Nevesely. **103 William Bowen:** (crb). **104 Alamy Stock Photo:** age

fotostock / Gonzalo Azumendi (cl). **104-105 Imagelibrary India Pvt Ltd:** Peng Shi. **106-107 Terrence Lee / Terenceleezy. 106 Alamy Stock Photo:** Design Pics Inc / John Hyde (cl). **108 Alamy Stock Photo:** Nature Picture Library (clb). **109 NASA:** NASA Earth Observatory maps by Joshua Stevens, using AMSR2 data supplied by GCOM-W1 / JAXA (r). **110-111 Getty Images:** Ben Cranke. **112-113 Getty Images:** Mark J. Thomas. **113 Getty Images:** Paul Souders (cr). **114-115 Joel A. Hagen. 114 Robert Harding Picture Library:** Matthias Baumgartner (cl). **116-117 Getty Images:** Anton Petrus. **117 Solent Picture Desk / Solent News & Photo Agency, Southampton:** (cr). **120-121 Rex Shutterstock:** AirPano. com / Solent News. **120 Getty Images:** Rieger Bertrand / hemis.fr (cl). **122-123 Alamy Stock Photo:** Aurora Photos / Ryan Deboodt. **122 John Spies:** (cl). **124-125 Getty Images:** Layne Kennedy. **124 Alamy Stock Photo:** WILDLIFE GmbH (bl). **126-127 Imagelibrary India Pvt Ltd:** Seth Aronstam. **126 Dreamstime.com:** Bragearonsen (cl). **128-129 Alamy Stock Photo:** Tom Till. **128 Alamy Stock Photo:** Tom Till (clb). **130-131 Getty Images:** John and Tina Reid. **131 Getty Images:** Funkystock (cr). **133 Dreamstime.com:** Andreas Wass (cr). **Getty Images:** D. Parer & E. Parer-Cook / Minden Pictures (bc). **134-135 Getty Images:** Andrew Watson. **136-137 Getty Images:** Universal Images Group. **137 Getty Images:** Majority World (crb). **138-139 Getty Images:** Jane Sweeney. **139 123RF.com:** alicenerr (crb). **140-141 Getty Images:** Yann Arthus-Bertrand. **140 Getty Images:** David Doubilet (cl). **142-143 Getty Images:** Anup Shah / Nature Picture Library. **142 Getty Images:** Paul & Paveena Mckenzie (cl). **146-147 Greg McCown / SaguaroPicture. 146 Alamy Stock Photo:** TravelStockCollection - Homer Sykes (cl). **148-149 Martin Rietze. 150-151 Sean R. Heavey. 150 Science Photo Library:** Paul D Stewart (cl). **152-153 Brian A. Morganti. 152 Getty Images:** Tasos Katopodis (clb). **154 Press Association Images:** John Locher / AP Photo (cl); AP Photo / John Locher (clb). **154-155 Chopperguy.com:** Photographer Jerry Ferguson, Pilot Andrew Park. **157 Getty Images:** Mario Tama (tr). **158-159 Alamy Stock Photo:** NOAA Handout / Gado. **160-161 Imagelibrary India Pvt Ltd:** Krzysztof Hanusiak. **161 Getty Images:** Guenter Fischer (crb). **162-163 Getty Images:** David McNew. **162 NSW Rural Fire Service:** (clb). **164-165 Getty Images:** Noppawat Tom Charoensinphon.

165 NASA: Imager for Magnetopause-to-Aurora Global Exploration (crb). **166-167 Press Association Images:** Biswaranjan Rout / AP. **167 Getty Images:** Sami Sarkis (crb). **168-169 Nasser Alomari. 168 Photoshot:** (clb). **172 Press Association Images:** AP Photo (cl). **172-173 Rex Shutterstock:** Dennis M. Sabangan / EPA. **174-175 Getty Images:** The Asahi Shimbun. **174 Rex Shutterstock:** Miyako City Officer (clb). **176-177 Getty Images:** Cultura RM Exclusive / Lost Horizon Images. **176 123RF.com:** Paolo Gianfrancesco (cl). **178-179 Alberto Garcia. 178 U.S. Geological Survey:** T. J. Casadevall (clb). **180-181 Alamy Stock Photo:** imageBROKER / Josef Beck. **182-183 Getty Images:** Paul Crock. **183 Getty Images:** William West / AFP (cr). **184-185 Getty Images:** Robyn Beck / AFP. **184 Getty Images:** Benjamin Lowy (cl). **186-187 123RF.com:** Manuel Perez Medina. **186 FLPA:** Photo Researchers (clb). **190-191 National Geographic Creative:** Frans Lanting. **192-193 naturepl.com:** Wim van den Heever. **193 Getty Images:** Martin Harvey (bc). **194-195 Dreamstime.com:** Jonmanjeot. **195 Alamy Stock Photo:** Cultura RM / Image Source (bc). **196-197 Alamy Stock Photo:** robertharding / Ian Egner. **196 naturepl.com:** Andy Sands (bl). **198-199 naturepl.com:** Bryan and Cherry Alexander. **198 Alamy Stock Photo:** Robert McGouey / Wildlife (bl). **200-201 Promote Iceland:** Ragnar Th. Sigurdsson. **201 Alamy Stock Photo:** age fotostock / Michael S. Nolan (bc). **202-203 SeaPics.com:** C & M Fallows. **202 Alamy Stock Photo:** GM Photo Images (bl). **204 Getty Images:** Tom Pfeiffer / VolcanoDiscovery (ftr); Andrew Watson (tr). **Robert Harding Picture Library:** Matthias Baumgartner (tc). **206 Alamy Stock Photo:** Minden Pictures (tc). **Getty Images:** Layne Kennedy (ftr); Martin Yon (tr). **208 Alamy Stock Photo:** Geoffrey Morgan (tr)

Front Endpapers: **Getty Images:** Yann Arthus-Bertrand 0; *Back Endpapers:* **Getty Images:** Yann Arthus-Bertrand 0

All other images © Dorling Kindersley
For further information see:
www.dkimages.com